Tamar

Tamar

A Story of Adventure, Intrigue, and
Romance in Ancient Israel

Glover Shipp

RESOURCE *Publications* • Eugene, Oregon

TAMAR
A Story of Adventure, Intrigue, and Romance in Ancient Israel

Copyright © 2014 Glover Shipp. All rights reserved. Except for brief quotations in critical publications or reviews, no part of this book may be reproduced in any manner without prior written permission from the publisher. Write: Permissions. Wipf and Stock Publishers, 199 W. 8th Ave., Suite 3, Eugene, OR 97401.

Resource Publications
An Imprint of Wipf and Stock Publishers
199 W. 8th Ave., Suite 3
Eugene, OR 97401

www.wipfandstock.com

ISBN 13: 978-1-62564-942-3

Manufactured in the U.S.A.   08/26/2014

Acknowledgments

I am grateful to many people for encouraging and helping me to write this novel. First, my wife Margie, always faithful, our son Mark, for his insights. He has devoted a number of years to the dig at Tamar and to research related to it. I am thankful to Linda Walts for reading the manuscript. I am thankful to Dr. DeWayne Coxon and his organization, Blossoming Rose, for providing a place to stay and meals at digs in which I participated at Tamar.

A special thank-you to Lauren Owsley and David Hardin, church friends in Edmond, Oklahoma, for posing for the cover art. I thank Matthew Wimer and the staff of Wipf and Stock for their invaluable aid in producing the book.

And I also wish to thank Yigal Israel and Tali Erickson-Gini, resident archeologists for the Israel Antiquities Authority, for the help and encouragement they gave me at the Tamar dig.

Contents

List of Illustrations | ix
Foreword | xi
Introduction | xv

scroll 1	Hanani's Roots	1
scroll 2	Conscripted!	8
scroll 3	Hanani's Pity Party	17
scroll 4	Time to Command . . . Sort of	25
scroll 5	First Brush with Danger	29
scroll 6	Mother of All Sandstorms	34
scroll 7	Captured!	36
scroll 8	Sela Has Unexpected Guests	43
scroll 9	Ba'ana's Revenge	48
scroll 10	An Affair of the Heart	55
scroll 11	Hanani's Heart on Hold	59
scroll 12	A Fugitive Seeks Shelter	63
scroll 13	Gold in Those Hills!	66
scroll 14	A Commitment of Love	69
scroll 15	The Lions Are out Tonight	77
scroll 16	The King Is Dead! Long Live the King!	81
scroll 17	Hanani Turns Smuggler	87
scroll 18	Hanani Has a Shadow	98
scroll 19	A New Assignment	102

Contents

scroll 20   First Test as Commander | 109
scroll 21   Hanani Takes a Bride | 116
scroll 22   Tamar Stricken | 123
scroll 23   An Attack Foiled | 128
scroll 24   Elohim's Hand on the Enemy | 132
scroll 25   Boundary Dispute | 137
scroll 26   An Unexpected Recall | 141
scroll 27   The Battle for Holy Ground | 146
scroll 28   Oh, My Hanani! | 152
scroll 29   Prisoners of War | 154
scroll 30   Nothing but Sand | 158
scroll 31   Reunited at Last! | 164

Glossary | 167

Illustrations

Hannah and Hanani | xviii

Map of Israel at the Time of Solomon | xix

Partial View of Tel Tamar: On-site Art by Author | xx

Solomon's Gates, Tamar: On-site Art by Author | xxi

Foreword

THE ANCIENT SITE OF biblical Tamar ('En Hazeva / Ain Husb) ranks among the most important archaeological sites in southern Israel. It is situated along an important route that stretched from Egypt, across Sinai and the central Negev Highlands down to the Arabah depression and the copper mines of Faynan, located on its eastern edge. This road reached the Arava Valley and biblical Tamar by way of the Scorpions Ascent, a significant landmark in ancient times.

In the first half of the first millennium BC, a series of fortifications were built next to the spring, which has since been identified as biblical Tamar. The initial use of the site appears to have been connected to the heavy volume of copper mining discovered in Khirbet Nahash in the Faynan region, between the eleventh and ninth centuries BC.

The precise date of the fortifications in biblical Tamar and the kings who ordered their construction are unknown but archaeological evidence points to their Judean origin in the time of the United Monarchy and the Kingdom of Judah. This evidence dovetails with the biblical account in which kings such as Solomon, Jehoshaphat and Uzziah strove to establish trade with Arabia and Africa by way of the Red Sea at Ezion-geber and Elath. The ceramic evidence of the later occupation of the site in the seventh and sixth centuries BC points to a significant Edomite presence: biblical Tamar was located only a day's journey from the Edomite capital of Busayra. This is precisely the time during which the Edomites were pressing deep into the southern Judah, a fact emphasized by written evidence discovered in the Judean fortress in Arad. The remains of a shrine with numerous buried cultic vessels were discovered directly outside the walls of biblical Tamar.

Foreword

Many of the vessels and other cultic objects found elsewhere in the site closely parallel those found in the Edomite shrine at Qitmit near Arad.

Judean control of the great fortress of biblical Tamar appears to have waned towards the end of the Judean kingdom, the demise of which was complete with the Babylonian conquest of Jerusalem in 587 BC.

Around the beginning of the first century AD the Nabataeans, an ancient people long established in Petra, began to use the site. In 106 AD the Nabataean kingdom was annexed by Rome and the site came under their control.

Massive construction took place above the ruins of the early fortress towards the end of the third century AD. At this time, the Roman emperor Diocletian revived copper mining in the Faynan region, where numerous Christians were consigned work and suffered in deplorable conditions. Under Diocletian, a fort with corner towers was constructed, along with a cavalry camp and military bathhouse. Small forts were established southeast of Tamar and along the road leading up the Scorpions Ascent towards Mampsis.

In 363 CE, the site was nearly demolished by a powerful earthquake that destroyed half of Petra and caused a trail of destruction throughout the region. The continued importance of Tamar in this period can be seen in the efforts expended to rebuild the fort and other structures, which was to remain in use another one hundred years, whereas other Roman forts in the Arava Valley were abandoned.

The site came back into use for a generation or two in the eighth century AD, when the region was under Islamic rule. In that period, families took advantage of springs in the arid region of the Arava Valley to grow crops. At Tamar, a family used the ruins of the bathhouse as a dwelling and built aqueducts in order to irrigate nearby fields.

Biblical Tamar remained abandoned for centuries until the British Mandate period after 1917. At that time, a new road to modern Eilat was constructed parallel to the Scorpions Ascent and the site was used as police station for the British camel corps patrolling the road between 'En Hazeva and Mampsis. Following the establishment of the State of Israel in 1948, the site was used for military purposes and eventually farming families settled there.

Archaeological remains at the site were first detected in 1902 by the Czech explorer, Alois Musil. T.E. Lawrence ("Lawrence of Arabia") described bubbling spring at the deserted site in his book, *Seven Pillars of Wisdom* (1922).

Foreword

The first excavations in biblical Tamar were carried out by Rudolph Cohen in 1972 on behalf of the Israel Dept. of Antiquities. The site was excavated extensively by Cohen and Yigal Israel on behalf of the Israel Antiquities Authority between 1987 and 1995. Following their excavations the site became an archaeological park managed and maintained by the Blossoming Rose Organization under the direction of Dr. DeWayne Coxon. Members of the organization participated in archaeological conservation courses conducted at the site and volunteers continue to carry out conservation in structures there, both ancient and modern.

More recently, excavations in the earliest part of the site near the spring were carried out on behalf of the Israel Antiquities Authority by Yigal Israel between 2005 and 2008 and by Tali Erickson-Gini in 2013. These excavations were conducted together with R.M. Shipp (Austin Graduate School of Theology), C. Bowman (Rochester College), T. Christian and a number of volunteers together with the aid of the Blossoming Rose Organization.

Dr. Tali Erickson-Gini
Institute of Archaeology
The Hebrew University of Jerusalem

Introduction

MY FIRST VIEW OF Tamar was at night. As our tour bus turned off the highway toward it, the tel appeared as if by magic, its contours lit up by spotlights. There was something awe-inspiring about the dark night, the silence of the desert and the mysterious mound before us. What secrets of the far past would it reveal?

As ancient ruins go, Tamar isn't all that big, but it holds much history in its many layers of construction, destruction and reconstruction. It received its name from the Hebrew word for date palm. We had learned that Tamar was a fortress from at least the time of Solomon. Above the ruins of Solomon's fortress were other fortresses attributed to King Uzziah of Judah in the 8th century, later expansions at an uncertain date, and then Nabatean and Roman installations in the first and second centuries AD. Below Solomon's era fortress, earlier ruins have been unearthed. Located in the desolate Negev of southern Israel, about 100 ancient miles (or 70 present miles) due south from Jerusalem, it was remote from any other settlement. Watered by a perpetual spring, it served as a border fortress and was at a strategic crossroads of caravan routes, marking one of the southern approaches to the more inhabited portions of Israel. In fact, it was located at a junction point of the famed Spice Road running from far-off India to the Mediterranean Sea and Egypt, and that of the road from Jerusalem to far-south Eilat on the Red Sea. Tamar is mentioned in the Old Testament and in Roman records, so it is an authentic historical site and is one of the best-preserved tels in all of Israel.

My son Mark, his colleague Craig Bowman, a group of fellow pilgrims and I descended from the bus and took a long look at what would be our

Introduction

desert home for the next few days. Tamar is well preserved, surrounded by an arid plain, an occasional lonely acacia tree, rocks strewn here and there, and, in the distance, a range of mountains. Everything is uniformly a nondescript brown or tan. Only part of the tel, constructed of bricks of the same drab color as its surrounding ground, has been unearthed and even less than that restored.

Off to the sides of the dig were two clusters of plain vanilla construction trailers, surrounded by a few palms, oleanders and other kinds of trees, a well and a modest central dining hall. Lugging our bags, we were herded to the trailers, grandly announced as our Tamar Hilton. Each trailer, in keeping with our environment, was named after one of the Israelite tribes. I was assigned to Judah, where I laid claim to a cot, one of several along both sides of a narrow aisle. Not much else adorned the room except a few posters of Israeli scenes. At one end was one of the world's smallest bathrooms, which included a postage-stamp-size shower.

Our group of tourists and archeologists was then called into the dining hall/kitchen area for orientation and a simple meal. It was prepared in strictly kosher style, as were all of our meals there. Never were meat and milk products served at the same time and, of course, no pork products were ever served. After dinner we were dismissed to our trailers. We were pretty pumped up, so it took some time for talking to slow down and sleep to come.

The next morning we were at breakfast early and then went on a brief tour of the tel, including the Roman ruins at the far end of the site. We visited what are called Solomon's Gates, an entranceway that was double-walled and imposing in size. We admired a giant, gnarled jujube tree, crowned with dark greenish-grey leaves. It is more than 2,000 years old and marks a spring that has bubbled up at that spot for eons of time, making it possible to survive there.

Then we received our assignments for the day. Some would work at sandbagging and otherwise maintaining the site. Some would help plant date palm trees on the property around the dig. Still others would actually get down into the trenches and search for whatever artifacts might come to light. One breakthrough came when we discovered the "kitchen" in a four-room house in ruins just outside of the fortress walls and near Solomon's Gates. Another "breakthrough" of sorts came when someone unearthed a Coca-Cola bottle cap buried in the debris! We surmised that it didn't date from Solomon's times.

Introduction

So went our first stay at Tamar. The next year we returned, this time with official permission to actually do more serious digging under the watchful eye of an Israeli archeologist with long experience in the region. Our digging took us down to the base of the walls of Solomon's original fortress. A few good pieces of pottery, cookware, a grain crushing stone, a perfume bottle and other items came to light, to our immense satisfaction.

Subsequent visits to the dig have further established the authenticity of the Solomonic fortress, as well as those above it and even below it. During a more recent dig, in 2007, the remains of a possibly earlier settlement of Midianite origin were found below the level of the 10th Century fortress. This indicated that the site may have been occupied even before the days of Solomon. Now, in 2013, yet another possible fortress was discovered, pushing the dating back to about 1200 BC.

My major tasks at the dig were to record in words, on film and in drawings the tel and whatever surfaced from our digging. As I sat there during the chilly high desert mornings making sketches and writing down our findings, I wondered just how those stationed there in the days of Solomon and following his time lived, what adventures they had and what dangers they faced. Out of my ponderings came the idea of writing a novel about this intriguing place and its occupants. My son Mark and his friend Terrance Christian, an archeologist in his own right, encouraged me to bring to life one warrior stationed at Tamar in the time of Solomon and his heir to the throne, Rehoboam.

Although most of the figures in the novel are fictional, I have attempted to make them real live people, with all of their trials and triumphs—people who trusted in God to deliver them. Happy reading about our hero, Hanani; his love, Hannah; and the other actors in our story. Hurt and rejoice with them. Hiss, if you wish, their enemies. This, then, is Hanani's story.

Are you ready for Hanani's adventures? Read on . . .

Hannah and Hanani

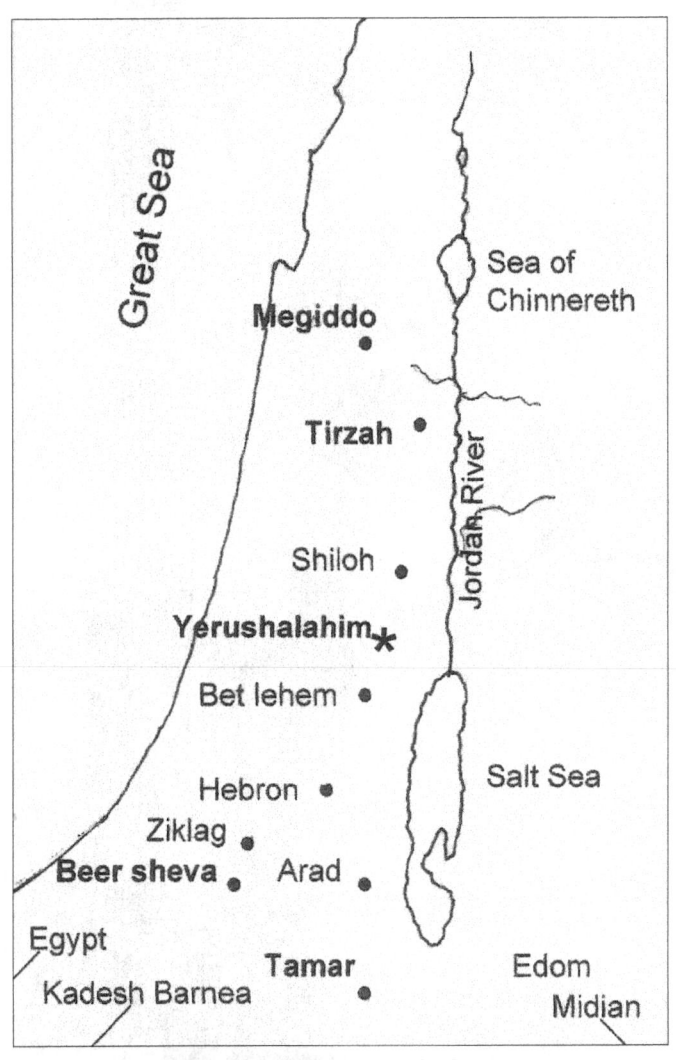

Map of Israel at the Time of Solomon

Partial View of Tel Tamar
On-site Art by Author

Solomon's Gates, Tamar

On-site Art by Author

scroll 1

Hanani's Roots

"This accursed heat! This scorching wind and sand!" moaned the young warrior Hanani ben Amran, as he stood atop the wall of Great King Solomon's fortress at Tamar, watching the wind kicking up sand and dust devils all about the fortress and the adjacent commander's house.

"Why is it my lot to spend three years in this infernal desert? There is nothing here worth defending. Who would even want to fight over our little pile of rock? This isn't what I signed up for! There is no adventure, no war, no nothing here! As far as I can see, all is sand, sand, sand . . . some dry and rocky hills in the distance, and a few scrubby acacia trees."

So went Hanani's daily complaint, especially during the scorching summer months, as he stood guard over the "pile of rocks" called a border fortress. During the winter the weather was cool, even chilly. But even then he grumbled, raising his arms to heaven and crying,

"O Adonai, why did you place me here? Except for the Sabbath and a few games under our flickering oil lamps, it's always the same! About the only relief is an occasional caravan that stops off here overnight. If we had any silver, we could buy a trinket or two from the traders, but we don't have a piece of silver to our name. Even our great King Solomon has forgotten us!"

"Isaac," he called out to a fellow guard, "how long has it been since we received any pay, rations or clothing?"

"I don't know," Isaac answered, "but our commander would know. Sir, when did we last receive any pay or provisions?"

Tamar

"Why do you want to know? Do you wish to write out a complaint? Oh, I forgot! You can't write! Besides, it is not for you to question such matters. In good time we will receive our allotments."

"Yes," grumbled Isaac, "about the time when our 'prison term' here is over."

With that exchange, Hanani went back to his interminable walking to and fro along the walls' parapets—a hundred boring paces here, a hundred there . . . all for nothing, because nothing ever seemed to happen to relieve the monotony of his "adventurous" military life.

Hanani was a young man of 18 from the fortress city of Megiddo, far north in the beautiful Jezreel Valley. By his time it already had a long history. Formerly a Canaanite stronghold, it had come eventually under the control of Israel. Because of its strategic location at the head of a pass through the Carmel Hills and adjacent to the well-traveled Way of the Sea, which led from Phoenicia on the north to Egypt on the south, it controlled access to the pass and valley. Whoever owned Megiddo owned the northern region of Israel. King Solomon had fortified it further and had located a large garrison of cavalry and chariots in its confines. Shaped roughly as an oval, the dark basalt stone fortress had a forbidding appearance, heavy and lofty against the sky. It had only one gate through its sturdy casemate wall, with its entrance ramp running sideways to the wall and then turning abruptly to the left just before it came to the heavy gate complex. This made it a challenge for an enemy chariot or siege engine to attack the gates. The solid casemate walls added to the difficulty of conquering the fortress.

Within the fortress proper there were simple, unadorned barracks, a central court, officers' quarters and stalls for the many chariot horses housed there. One area was heaped high with provender for the horses. There was also a work area, where chariots were repaired, horses shoed, harness repaired and maintenance done on armor and weapons. Water was obtained through an underground series of tunnels and basins, connected to a distant stream. The fortress was pretty much self-contained, which was good insurance against enemy attacks, which occurred fairly frequently.

Actually, Hanani's home was outside of Megiddo. He lived with his family on a small farm near the fortress, a plot of land handed down from his ancestors. Situated on a low mound about 2,000 paces from Megiddo's gates, the farm had an unobstructed view of the distant range extending southward from rocky Mt. Carmel, jutting out toward the sea, and the fertile Jezreel Valley reaching to the rounded shape of Mt. Gilboa, site of the tragic death in battle of King Saul and his sons.

"Shalom, traveler, stop and rest under our trees," shouted out Amram ben Uziel, master of his home and holdings. "Drink in the tranquil scene before you. And sip a cup of our own wine."

"Shalom in return," the visitor answered. "It would be a pleasure to spend a few moments with you. The day is hot."

Gnarled olive trees, garbed in their green-grey gowns, shimmered in a gentle breeze. Rows of grapevines marched across the landscape. Here and there were clusters of pomegranate trees, their bright red fruit punctuating their leafy foliage. Farther up in the foothills sycamore fig trees fought with almonds and cypresses for space. Toward the top of the range were stately oaks, spreading their branches wide for shade-seeking birds and beasts, and anchoring the hills with their deep-seated roots.

"What a splendid little farm you have," the guest commented. "I see that you have terraced it well."

"Yes, terracing helps hold the soil and mulch in place and makes for fairly level areas for crops. With much hard work and family cooperation, our inheritance has become productive. We grow wheat, barley, beans, onions, lentils and even watermelons. Our olive trees are yielding well. We also grow figs, grapes and pomegranates. My flock is small, but adequate for our needs for milk, wool and occasional meat. All in all, most of what the family consumes is produced in our own fields."

"Very good, my friend. Allow me to introduce myself. I am Jediael ben Zechariah, from Kinnereth, of the tribe of Naphtali, on the way to Joppa on business."

"And I am Amran ben Uziel, of the tribe of Manasseh. It is late in the day. Come pass the night in our humble home."

"You are most generous, Amran ben Uziel. May our great Elohim repay you for your hospitality."

"Rachel," Amran called to his wife, "we will have a guest for the night."

"Very well, my husband," she answered from inside the house. "Carmi," she called to her oldest daughter, "come help me prepare our meal. We have a guest."

Tamar

The farm boasted a modest four-room dwelling, of the kind typical throughout Israel. The house, built of native basalt stone, was made sufficiently sturdy to support a second floor, but the family's means were so minimal that this "luxury" had never been realized. The structure was enclosed by a walled courtyard, which contained a threshing floor about 10 spans across, a well, wine and olive oil presses, and a beehive-shaped oven.

Speaking of beehives, except in bad weather, the courtyard was a beehive of activity. Females of the family had the daily tasks of drawing water, grinding grain, kneading and baking bread, and, during harvest time, stomping knee-deep in grapes, crushing them down to liquid, skin and seeds. Some grapes they dried on mats facing the sun. The dark crimson nectar of the crushed grapes was fermented and processed into wine, a family staple. Olives were pressed by squeezing them into a tub with a large wooden screw turned by hand to extract the precious oil. It was then filtered and placed in clay jars for future use in cooking, for providing fuel for lamps and for soothing a variety of skin ailments.

"Girls," Rachel would call out frequently, "if you have finished toting water, it is time to get back to our weaving."

"Yes, mother," they chorused, as they continued to dally along the path to the family well.

The house itself had one door and four small windows, two on each side. Entering through the doorway, a visitor would see a long corridor open to the sky. To the left were storage rooms and sleeping quarters. At the back was a cooking area, with more space for storage. A fire pit was about six spans across and was lined with stones. Meat, seldom served except on festive occasions, such as during Passover or when visitors graced the home, was slowly roasted on a spit over hot coals. Other food items, such as lentils, were placed in earthenware bowls and allowed to simmer over the coals. Rachel devoted hours a day to preparing food, as she squatted over the fire pit, keeping the fire stoked and the food cooking as uniformly as possible. Its smell might have been pleasant, except for the smoke drifting up into her face and drowning out any fragrance. She didn't complain about her lot, however. It was the same as that of any other farm wife in Israel.

To the right of the central corridor was an area housing domestic animals during the winter or in bad weather. The stench from the animals' droppings could be heavy, but families were accustomed to it. Hay and grain were stored in that area, easily accessible for replenishing the feeding troughs.

The flat roof was constructed of rough cypress or oak logs, overlaid with smaller branches, palm fronds, grasses and a thick coating of clay. In compliance to a command in their sacred law, a low parapet was required, to protect those on the roof from falling off. The roof, very important to daily life, was often frequented after the workday during the warm season. Cool breezes drifted across it at night, making it a comfortable place in which to gather and even to sleep. A narrow stairway outside of the house itself led to the roof.

The home's furnishings were sparse and consisted of a low table, cushions, some cowhide floor mats to cover the earthen floor, bows, spears, walking staffs and a prized copy of the Shema on a tiny parchment scroll. There were fire-blackened pots for cooking, a handful of tongs and other kitchen utensils, several large jars for storage of water and grain, three oil lamps and stands for them, bed mats for each of the family members, hooks on the walls for robes and little else.

"Go call the boys from the fields." she said to her younger daughter, Dinah. "Our repast is about ready."

"Yes, my mother," she answered as she skipped out of the house and through the gate.

"Come, Jediael, and join us for our meal," Amran said to his guest. He washed his hands in a basin Carmi provided for him. Then he was motioned to a cushion to the right of Amran's.

"Ah, here are my sons," Amran announced, as the boys stormed into the house. "This is my oldest, Hanani, followed by Gunih, Hezron and Serah."

"It is a pleasure to meet you," Jediael told them.

"And it is a pleasure to know you, honored Jediael," Hanani spoke for the boys.

"Let us bow before our great God," Amran said. "O Elohim, Provider of all that exists, we thank you for the provision of this food. We thank you for our home and family, and especially, for our guest. Amen."

"Amen and amen," added Jediael.

It was the universal custom for those eating to recline on cushions or sit on the floor, dipping their hand into the pots of food, using a crust of bread as a sop. They washed their hands ceremonially in a bowl of water before eating and again after the meal was finished. A towel was passed from person to person, to dry their hands. To signal that they were through eating, they would sop out their bowl with a piece of bread and then turn the bowl upside down.

Tamar

As the meal ended, Amran reminded his family that the next day was preparation day for the Sabbath.

"As is our custom, Jediael, our women prepare food tomorrow for the Sabbath. Our boys give extra fodder and water to the animals, to tide them over the Sabbath. You are welcome to remain over the morrow and the Sabbath," he told Jediael, "if you so choose."

"You are most gracious, but I must be on my way on the morrow."

After a hurried morning repast, Jediael left, saying, "Shalom on this house."

Amran responded, "Shalom be on you, too. May you travel under Elohim's protective wing. And now, boys, back to the fields."

"Ah, father," Hezron asked, "since this is the preparation day for the Sabbath, why don't we prepare in spirit for the morrow by resting and meditating today?"

"If you mean, son," Amran answered, "that you can just lie around all day, that will not serve. This is a day of work, not rest, so let us get to work."

Hanani ben Amran was the firstborn son of Amran ben Uziel and Rachel bani Gaddiel. His younger siblings were Gunih, 17; Hezron, 15; Serah, 13; Carmih, 10; and Dinah, 7—three other boys and two girls. Most of Amran's daylight hours, except for the Sabbath, were spent in farming. Hanani's role was to act as organizer of family work details, which he relished.

"Hey, Gunih, quit lazing around and put your back into carrying those stones!" he would yell.

"And who made you my overseer?" Gunih answered sarcastically.

"It is my right as the oldest son," Hanani responded harshly. "Besides, Father told me to keep you on the job." What a pleasure it was to command his younger siblings!

With a good build, curly black hair and dark eyes, Hanani was already catching the secret glances of the girls in their region. He had learned to read and write at the feet of a priest and that set him apart. Few boys and no girls of his age learned to master the written tongue. Only by insisting to his parents that he could become literate was he finally permitted time each week to go to the local priest for instruction.

"Father," he implored, "please let me learn to read and write. I know I can and it will benefit me in the future."

"Why?" Amran asked. "You don't need learning all of that to farm. You just need a strong back and a will to succeed."

"Father . . . " he started again with his reasons for wanting to become literate.

"My boy," Amran said, as he put his arm around his son, "we will discuss it further with your mother."

Finally, after Hanani's much wearing them down, his parents agreed to allow him to become literate. Off he went in search of the priest, and was soon engulfed in learning the letters and word structure of their Hebrew tongue.

Hanani didn't know exactly what he wanted to do with his life, but it wasn't to stay at home. He longed to see the world—or at least the Land of Israel. He had been to distant Jerusalem for feast days, but beyond that, he had never traveled anywhere. Yet he dreamed of far places, places he had heard about from traders or travelers.

"One day I'm going to visit some of those countries," he vowed. "What fun it would be to travel to Tyre and Sidon, Egypt and far-off Tarshish. Perhaps I could even become wealthy in some kind of trade with those lands."

Then suddenly his opportunity came to see the world, or at least a little of it.

scroll 2

Conscripted!

ONE DAY AN AGENT of the Great King arrived at Hanani's humble home and was received by Rachel. Surprised, she asked,

"Sir, what do you wish of us?"

"I am here to conscript your son Hanani for three years of mandatory service to our king. Is he here?"

"No, Sir, but I will send someone to call him in from the fields."

Hanani soon arrived, out of breath from running,

"Hanani ben Amran?" the agent spoke up. "You are hereby required to serve our Great King Solomon for three years. You may either work on our king's construction projects or enroll in the military. It is one or the other."

"I choose to be a warrior," Hanani announced, after only a moment's pause. "It will be a lot more fun than hoisting blocks of stone around. I know how backbreaking that is. Besides, since there aren't any wars going on right now, I'll be safe."

"But, son," Amran said, "our people are farmers. That is all you know. Besides, you are our firstborn. Your responsibility is to care for our inheritance and pass it on to your firstborn. This is Elohim's plan for Israel. It is your task to maintain our land. Since you must serve our king for a period of time, then ask to be assigned to his royal gardens right here in the valley. In that way we can be together frequently, you can keep an eye on our farm and we will know you are faring well."

"Father, I would like to honor your request. I would like to care for our land, but my mind is made up. A warrior's life is for me. Besides, farming doesn't suit me at all. I have bigger things in mind for my life."

"Bigger things, son? What can be more important than working the soil?"

"A lot of things, father. For one, with my literary ability, I can become a scribe for our king, or a public servant in some other capacity. I can prepare to be sent as an emissary to other lands. Oh, there is much I can do besides plowing up our pitiful little plot of land."

Further argument by his father proved fruitless. His parents regretted at that moment their earlier decision to allow Hanani to study.

"Now his head is full of all kinds of dreams," Rachel moaned. "He just had to learn all that business of reading and writing! Now he wants to see the world about which he has read. He even wants to live in our great king's palace."

"Here is your notice of conscription, Hanani ben Amran," the agent explained. "Present it tomorrow at the third hour of the day to the fortress gate guard at Megiddo.

The next morning Hanani finally tore himself away from his tearful mother and downcast father. His siblings clung to him. He was their hero, going off to "war."

"Bring us back something you took from our enemies!" they pleaded. Hanani laughed, tousled their hair and then packed up his simple belongings—a change of clothing, his robe, a sharpening stone for his knife, bow and arrows, sling, bed mat and a few potions that his mother insisted that he take with him to ward off illness . . . as if he would ever become ill! He hugged his mother again and, clasping his father's arms, bid him a solemn farewell.

"Shalom, my father. Take good care of our family. Mother, pray for me. And you young ones . . . behave yourselves and obey your father and mother."

He then hoisted his pack, picked up his staff, looked back once at his forlorn family and went running toward Megiddo. It didn't take him long to make the journey. Arriving at its massive gates, he was summarily stopped in his tracks.

"Halt!" called out a sentry. "What business do you have here, boy?"

"Sir, I'm here to report for military duty. This is the conscription notice our great king's agent gave me."

"Alright, but I don't see why the agent would want to sign you up for the military. You look like a common farmhand to me. What is this army coming to? Oh, well, I will take it to my commander. Wait here!"

He came back soon and told Hanani to follow him.

"So you are one of our new conscripts?" Commander Yigal asked. "First, can you read?

"Yes, Sir!"

"Is this your name—Hanani ben Amran?"

"Yes, Sir, that is my name."

"Where is your home, Hanani?"

"Very near, Sir. Our lands are toward the sea, on a knoll overlooking the valley."

"I see. Now what can you do besides read and write, and, I assume, care for farmlands?"

"Sir, I am adept at using both the sling and the bow."

"Very good. We will soon test you on these weapons and teach you to use others. You will receive details on our training schedule, meals and duties while here. Dismissed. Aide, take ben Amran to the barracks and assign him a space."

"Yes, Commander. Now come with me, farm boy."

Hanani was soon in a cold and dark stone barracks, where he was assigned a skimpy bed mat that looked the worse for wear. He opted to place his own bed mat on top of it, so as to have a degree of comfort as he slept.

"Man, with all of the wealth our great king has, you would think that he could provide better beds than this!" he exclaimed.

A fellow conscript, Joab, told Hanani,

"This is just part of the military's way of making warriors suffer. You will get used to it."

"I did expect something a little better," Hanani confessed.

Hooks on the wall by his mat held a parade robe and tunic, a utilitarian robe, a helmet, leather armor, an archery set, a short sword and scabbard, and a shield. A leather bag contained extra sandals, boots, leather leggings and arm protectors, a carving knife, unguents and cloth bands for wounds. He examined each item carefully.

Conscripted!

"This parade uniform will make me the envy of all the girls," he chuckled. "And I can't wait to try out my armor and weapons. This will be fun!"

"Sure it will!" Joab said, a bit sarcastically.

Hanani was eager to begin his training. He had been treated so cordially by officers upon arrival that he expected the same "royal treatment" to continue. How wrong he was! His first early morning call was to a simple but adequate meal. Then he joined a handful of other recruits. They faced a burly officer who roared like an angry lion.

"Alright, you miserable excuses for manhood! You ignorant clods! You are going to regret every day of your training. Now line up! No, no, no! In a straight line! You do know what a straight line is, don't you? That's a little better. Now, shed all of your extra weight and come to the gate. We are going to get some exercise in the brisk outdoor air."

The recruits meekly obeyed and were soon gathered together just outside of the gate.

"Now, run to Gilboa," the officer commanded, "and keep going all the way to the top. Once there, descend rapidly. No, that isn't all. You will turn around and repeat the process. Anyone who stops will make the circuit a third time!"

"But, Sir," complained one of the conscripts, "I am not used to such arduous work. I am a potter by trade."

"So? That's all the more reason for you to get into shape for military service. Now get to running, all of you!"

He and the other trainees grumbled at this and other exercises, but that made no difference to the officer in charge. In fact, the more complaining, the more demanding became the training.

Rigorous physical drills and forced marches were the order of the day, when the troops were not learning the discipline that the military required and practicing the art of warfare. Hanani soon picked up the use of the spear, lance and short sword. By the third day he was in practice contests with his fellow warriors, where he showed exceptional ability with the bow and sling. He could unerringly hit targets hanging from trees and his officers noted this.

"Warrior," commented Commander Yigal, "you have turned out to be one of the best recruits in this class. Congratulations! I will expect great things from you, both as a warrior and as a scribe."

"Thank you, Commander," Hanani answered. "That is praise, indeed, for I understand your standards are exceptionally high."

Tamar

Finally the moment came when Hanani and the other draftees "graduated" from basic training and were ready to leave Megiddo. All were garbed in their new dress tunics bearing the royal insignia. Their polished leather armor and brass helmets glistened in the sun. Their red dress robes were draped over their shoulders. Their swords were in place and their lances were in hand, the detachment insignia fluttering from the tops of the lances. Each carried on his back a large roll containing a bed mat, a utilitarian robe, a uniform for everyday use, extra sandals, boots, a repair kit for his sandals and clothing, salves and bandages, a food knife, a bowl, a combat knife and a "good luck" benediction from the Torah, which read,

> The Lord bless you and keep you;
> The Lord make his face shine upon you
> And be gracious to you;
> The Lord turn his face toward you
> And give you peace.

Each warrior was ready for whatever adventures lay ahead. Hanani awkwardly embraced his solemn father, tearful mother and younger brothers and sisters, who had come to see him off. His mother was especially distraught by his leaving.

"My son," she said, "please be careful and go with Elohim's blessings. We will miss you terribly."

"Don't worry about me, dear mother," he answered. "I know how to take care of myself."

Then he heard the shout from Commander Yigal, "Move out!" The troop strutted out of Megiddo and turned south toward Jerusalem. Once on the road they laughed and joked among themselves. It was good to be free of family restraints and ready for their great adventures ahead.

Southward the troop went through the Jezreel Valley and into the hill country of central Israel. It was springtime and the fields were a lush green. The Rose of Sharon was decked out in its finest dress. What a wonderful season it was and what a wonderful time to be ascending slowly upward toward Jerusalem, the Holy City!

The fledgling warriors' first night was spent in the rolling landscape near Dothan, situated in the heart of a broad valley, with rich red soil that produced a variety of crops and boasted some of the finest grazing lands in all Israel. This was a welcome relief from the white chalky hills through which they had just tramped. They built a campfire, unrolled their bed mats, ate a sparse meal of flat cakes, roasted grains of wheat, dried figs and wine, and

Conscripted!

then settled down for sleep. That night and each night during their travels Yigal posted a two-man guard, rotating this duty among them. They were not so much fearful of human predators as they were of the four-legged kind. Lions, bears, jackals and wolves were known to roam those hills.

At each village they passed local boys ran out to swagger with them for a ways, whooping it up.

"Hup! Hup! Hup! When I grow up, I'm going to be a famous warrior just like you!" one gangly youth announced importantly. "How many enemies have you killed?" "Are you going to war?" "Let me try out your sword."

"Oh, we're very famous," Commander Yigal joked with them. "Haven't you heard of the 'mighty men' of Megiddo?' We haven't killed any enemies yet, but we may. No, you can't try out our swords. You might cut your foot off!"

"I'll wager with you that I can sling a stone better and farther than any of you!" a husky youth yelled out.

"That so?" Hanani said. "Sir," he asked the commander, "may we stop for a moment and put this to the test?"

"I think we need to make this young man a bit more humble," Yigal answered.

All stopped, placing a stone in their slings, but allowed the boastful youth a first try. His shot was fairly impressive. Then, on Yigal's command, all of the warriors fired. With no exceptions, their stones flew considerably farther than his.

"Sorry, son," he told the crestfallen boy, "you will get better with age and practice. Now, warriors, let us resume our march."

Each day saw the troop climbing steadily along rough and rocky trails toward Solomon's great capital. They passed near Tirzah, a village that would figure significantly in Hanani's future. The weather was springtime warm. They continued through the fertile Dothan Plain, with its rich red earth. Hanani examined it as he walked along, commenting, "What a blessed land this is! I would guess that it could grow almost anything. And it is so rich in our history—the place where Jacob's sons were grazing their flocks, when young Joseph, ever the dreamer, happened onto them and was sold into Egyptian slavery."

As they marched along, they left the plains and climbed slowly. The Central Highlands, often chalky-white with limestone outcroppings, became more arid, with fewer farms and only scattered trees. Rocks strewed the landscape, that is, those that had not been utilized in building the countless terraces that curved around the hills. The terraces held back moisture and furnished relatively flat spaces for olives, sycamore figs, grapevines and other annual fruit producers. More and more flocks of sheep and goats were seen grazing on patches of grass. Most often they were tended by shy young girls, who guided their charges away from the warriors.

"Hey, little one!" one of the troopers shouted. "What are you called?"

This only caused the maiden to blush and hurry still farther away, as the men laughed boisterously. The contingent passed Shechem, nestled between Mt. Ebal and Mt. Gerizim, and on to Shiloh and Bethel, all famous in their national history, as they wound their way along the backbone of the Hill Country. Hanani had learned from his reading something of the significance of several of these towns in the Highlands.

"Shechem is where our great military ancestor Joshua, had the law read to the people. Shiloh is where the tabernacle and Sacred Ark of the Covenant were located for a long time before the temple was constructed," he explained to his cohorts. "They remained there until the great King David brought them to Jerusalem. Bethel is where our ancestor Jacob dreamed of angels ascending and descending a ladder reaching to the highest heavens. It is where he received the renewed promise that his people would one day inherit this entire land. He was so in awe of his vision that he named it Bethel, because he realized that it was a sacred place—the house of Elohim Himself."

"How do you know all of this?" asked one companion, Abdias.

"I learned how to read, so our priest let me sit down and carefully open his scrolls. I read it for myself."

"I wish I could read," Abdias answered.

"Well, perhaps I can teach you during our off-duty time."

"Do you think I could really learn?"

"If I could, I don't see why you couldn't."

Their march brought them toward evening on the fifth day to Jerusalem. They came over a ridge north of the city and there it was, spread out before them in the late afternoon sun. Most of the squad had never been there, so they stared open-mouthed at the splendor of the Temple and royal palaces. The temple complex, located on a high point above the city itself, had been constructed on a sacred plot of land that mighty King David had purchased. Brilliant in its near-white marble surfaces and gold inlay, the temple glittered like a huge diadem. Within the temple's massive walls and in front of the two great bronze pillars marking the entrance into the Holy Place, stood the altar, always ablaze with sacrifices to Elohim. To its side was a large brass laver, where the priests washed themselves, and smaller basins for cleansing the animals to be sacrificed.

"Look, everyone" excitedly shouted one in their group who had seen it before. "Nothing can compare with our glorious temple anywhere! I heard that every stone you see was carved out at a quarry and done so perfectly that no cutting or chiseling had to be done once it arrived on the Temple mount. And a vast quantity of gold and precious stones was used in its construction, provided by our great king David. Solomon lavished much of his own wealth on the temple."

"That's true," exclaimed Hanani, who had traveled to the city with his family for some of the great annual feasts. "It is so majestic and holy, glistening like a crown jewel! Our Great King spared nothing to make it the most beautiful house of worship ever built."

They stopped for a few moments of admiration and prayerful reflection on what the Temple meant to their people. It was the center of their life, the place where YHVH Himself dwelt within the most sacred Holy of Holies. To these hallowed grounds came thousands of pilgrims each year for the celebration of Passover, Pentecost, Atonement and Booths.

After taking in the beauty of the temple and its surrounding structures, the Megiddo squad approached the massive north wall, strode through the Fish Gate's double-walled entrance and into the city itself. Their route took them alongside the Temple Mount's western retaining wall, soaring upward and constructed of huge cut stones. Then passing by the magnificent royal palace complex, they hoped for a glimpse of the aged king himself or of some of his wives, but saw no one except guards along the outer walls.

"Man," commented Hanani, "I would love to catch a glimpse of the Great King's harem beauties. Is it true that he has hundreds of them?"

"So I hear," answered his friend Joab. "It seems a shame that we have no women and he has a horde of them. Oh, well, those royal ladies would never even look our way, so no use daydreaming about them."

"Still," said Hanani, "I would like to see at least one of them."

Winding their way along narrow and at times steep cobbled streets, they caught the watchful eye of shopkeepers and the attention of the inevitable mob of young boys, surrounding them and at times impeding their march. Their progress was also slowed by a sudden rainstorm that blew in horizontally and rendered the paving stones dangerously slick. They slipped and slid along up a series of steps, with a couple of the warriors falling and skinning knees and elbows.

"Hey, you farm boys, don't you know how to climb city steps?" shouted Yigal. "Be more careful."

The fledglings finally arrived at an austere limestone citadel, adjacent to the temple courtyard, where they would remain for a brief time before receiving their future assignments. They looked for all the world like half-drowned chickens. The fortress commander took one look at them and commented,

"I have never seen a sorrier bunch of warriors. I hope you clean up alright. If you don't, woe be to the future of our armed forces! Now follow me."

They were escorted to another drab barracks, where they laid out their bed mats and hung up their soaked garments and weapons.

"So far, not bad at all," commented Hanani. "We have seen some wonderful things. The march has not been difficult. Our food is plain but edible. Our 'royal inn' is just as comfortable as the one at Megiddo. And now we can enjoy a rest here in the Holy City." Rest? Very little, as it turned out.

Scroll 3

Hanani's Pity Party

The troopers had one day of leisure in which to strut around the narrow alleyways of the city. Some of them had never seen such a variety of items for sale. There were little stalls along every wall—cloth and other goods from distant lands, foods they had never before tasted, jewelry . . . They would have bought some trinkets, but had no coins. They did ogle several slim young girls, who gave them occasional admiring glances from over their veils.

The next morning the unit was called out early and presented to Hoshea, the commander of the border fortress at distant Tamar. He announced,

"Warriors, you are to accompany me to Tamar, where you will be stationed. We will leave at first light tomorrow, so be prepared. Make sure your sandals are sturdy, for the way is rough in places."

"Sir, where is Tamar?" asked Joab. "Never heard of it."

"It is five days' hard march from here. It is located in the eastern Negev as it faces the Arabáh. You will learn all about it in a few days. Now dismissed. Get a good rest tonight, for you will need your energy for the journey."

"The Negev?" asked Hanani. "Isn't that pretty much desert?"

"Actually very much, warrior. However, in some places there is vegetation, like along wadis or where there are springs. Tamar is hot and dry or cold and dry, depending on the season."

Tamar

"From my reading I recall that Tamar's value is that of its strategic location."

"Correct. It is at an important junction of the Spice Road and the road from Jerusalem to Ezion-geber on the Red Sea. I take it you can read and write."

"Yes, Sir."

"I will keep that in mind. Your ability may come in handy."

"This is not what I imagined our tour of duty would be," mumbled Hanani, as he headed with the others into the barracks.

No, it wasn't. Tamar was one of the least impressive of all of Solomon's fortresses and the only one that wasn't surrounded by a small village. And it was in an arid region, as Commander Hoshea had informed them. Yet, it was an important outpost on the southern flank of Israel, facing always-dangerous Edom to the east, Amalek and Midian to the south, and farther to the southwest, powerful Egypt.

The next day saw twenty-six troopers, the Megiddo contingent and one additional recruit from Shechem on their way south. They passed the village of Bethlehem, the ancient home of Solomon's illustrious father, David. It was small and nestled on rolling hills. The countryside around Bethlehem was rocky, but offered good grazing for sheep. They then continued in a southwestern direction through the Hebron Valley, the route the much earlier twelve spies, sent out by the noble Moses, had used to research the land of Canaan. Hanani gave a running commentary about this village:

"Hebron was the home for many years of our father Abraham, who was buried here, along with his wife Sarah; his son Isaac; Isaac's wife, Rebekah; Jacob and Leah. This is truly holy ground."

Their march took them southward past the small fortress at Araor and on to the precipitous Scorpion Ascent. As they stood for a moment at its top, Hanani took a long look at what lay ahead, down into the huge Ramón Crater.

"Man, as far as I can see," he muttered, "there is nothing ahead but desolate cliffs, a lot of rocks and a wadi or two. And it is a long way down to the bottom of it, if it has a bottom."

Hoshea ordered his men to descend, but carefully.

"It is treacherous going," he told them, "with a lot of loose shale. And by the way, it is not named Scorpion for nothing. Those little insects pack a terrible sting. And we may see an occasional serpent of the poisonous variety."

Hanani's Pity Party

They filed slowly, slipping and sliding downward, and finally reached the bottom, with only a few turned ankles, and were ever-watchful for those evil little scorpions. Then they headed eastward toward Tamar. Progress was still difficult, due to sharp rocks and gravel on what passed for a trail. And it was oppressively hot!

"I hope I never have to climb this pass," Hanani said to his companions. "Going down is treacherous enough. With every step we could lose our footing and tumble down the slope like a dislodged stone. It would be a monster to climb!" Little did he know that he would climb it many times in the future.

As they slowly made their way through the crater, they wondered about the seashells scattered here and there on the desert floor. They asked Hoshea,

"Sir, how did these seashell get here?"

"Sorry, warriors, but I don't know."

Beyond this hellhole, the daytime temperature became hotter and drier, so they had a good idea before arriving there what to expect at Tamar. The thought of it wasn't pretty! But as evening came on in the high desert, the air cooled down quickly, much to their relief.

One thing that constantly preoccupied them was lack of water. What they carried in skins had to last until the next spring or pond. Commander Hoshea warned them against guzzling it. If they did so, he said, they would suffer from thirst later on.

The troop passed high rock outcroppings, reddish-brown or ochre in color. There was nothing else to relieve the monotonous landscape, which looked as if Satan himself had created it. Not even a tree or blade of grass relieved the view before them.

Their evening stops were wherever they could find shelter from the chill of the night and its often harsh winds. For the most part they searched out shallow caves or the shelter of rocky cliffs. One night they enjoyed the bliss of a welcome oasis replete with a pond and several palm trees.

"Ah! How good it is to soak my burning feet in the water," sighed Hanani, "even though it is lukewarm, and to wiggle my toes in the welcome grass."

As usual, Commander Hoshea assigned guards, rotating the duty into watches, three men per watch. This oasis attracted both animals and humans, some decidedly unfriendly.

Tamar

"Keep a sharp eye out for predators," he ordered, "both the four-legged kind and the two-legged kind."

Nothing untoward happened during their continued journey. Near evening on the fifth day Hoshea and his warriors arrived at the fortress of Tamar. All of the recruits were genuinely disappointed. There it was in the middle of nowhere, standing alone in a nearly featureless landscape, except for some distant dry and rocky mountains. It was a small, stark complex with a triple entrance gate, casemate walls and a barracks located between the outer and inner walls along one side of the fortress. A sad little cluster of trees—an already-ancient jujube and some palms—huddled around the spring at the back of the fortress that was the real key to survival at Tamar.

The commander's home was just outside of the entrance gate complex, It was a larger than normal four-room house, laid out just like Hanani's home, but with a second floor. It was enclosed by a low wall, with a gate facing the entrance ramp to the fortress. It and the fortress were constructed of limestone blocks, cut out of the foothills. At least the limestone was less foreboding than the basalt blocks in their country. Inside the fortress itself were a command cubicle, storage rooms, the usual cheerless barracks, stalls for horses and mules, if they had any, and for the little herd of goats that was part of the fortress's meager holdings. Two sentry's towers, built above the entrance gates, overlooked the complex and surrounding area.

And that was it! Little vegetation was to be seen outside of the fortress, apart from an occasional gnarled acacia tree dotting the distant landscape and bent tortuously by vicious desert winds.

"This will be no adventure, but more like a prison term," Hanani grumbled.

It didn't take long for the conscripts to begin finding everything that was wrong about the place, just as soldiers have always done.

"It is too hot!" they griped. "It is too dry! It is too windy! There is little real shade! There is nothing to do here!" "The food is tasteless!" Ah, this was their major complaint!

"Our cook must have been a refugee from a stables somewhere!" the warriors agreed. "It is fare even goats would spurn."

They didn't at all like the warriors already there—a grumpy bunch who disdained them. Finally, there was nothing to do besides taking guard duty, shepherding the fortress's little flock of goats, foraging for grass for the two mules the commander maintained, playing games such as mancala, and sleeping.

Hanani's Pity Party

"Horrible outpost of Sheol!" was Hanani's daily complaint during the summer months as he guarded the fortress and its approach roads. One led south from Jerusalem to Ezion-geber, a port and fishing village on the Red Sea. The other led from Sela, the Edomite stronghold to the east and then on northwest to Gaza, the Philistine city near the coast of the Great Sea, or directly to the Way of the Sea and on down to Egypt. As Hanani had read earlier, Tamar was located at a crossroads, protecting the southern flank of Israel. However, that did not relieve his hatred of the place.

To cap off his revulsion, one day Hanani received additional orders.

"Hanani," Hoshea called out. "Today you have dung duty."

"Dung duty? You mean manure?"

"Exactly! Scoop up all of the animals' droppings and spread them out to further dry. Have you not noticed that they are fuel for our cooks' fires?"

"But, Sire, I fled the farm because I hated picking up dung."

"You are going to love doing it here, If not, you will still do it."

"Very well, but it is slaves' work."

"Of course it is, but that's what all of you are—lowly slaves of the military system."

"Grumble, grumble . . . " Hanani said to himself as he headed over to the animal stalls and then out into the area where the goats cropped whatever they could find to eat in the sandy soil.

They all endured the summer and longed for relief, which finally came in the tenth month. The wintertime night and morning watches were subject to cold desert winds. Hanani didn't mind that so much, because he at least had a warm cloak.

"But still," he moaned, "what a dreary place this is! The nearest decent settlements are Arad and Beersheba, but they are several days' journey away."

The village of Avdat was closer in distance, but still the traveler had to first pass by an unwelcoming Edomite village. Or he could descend into the devilishly hot below-sea-level Arabáh and then climb into the Eastern Highlands, eventually to arrive at Sela. It, too, was inhabited by Edomites, people unfriendly toward Hanani's people, even though they were related through their mutual ancestor Isaac.

Hanani complained about everything, but was not alone in his criticism. He was joined by a contingent of chronic complainers and one commander. Half of the total force had already been at Tamar for a year, so had developed a high sense of indignation about the place. For all Hanani knew, Commander Hoshea may have complained also, but no one except his wife would have known it. Hanani had heard that she was bitterly opposed to their being stationed there and he could sympathize with her. She had been brought there from Jerusalem after Hoshea had arrived at the fortress. At this tiny outpost she could not go to market or visit any women friends.

"That would drive any woman to the verge of insanity," Hanani suspected.

Hoshea and his wife had a half-dozen kids, usually scrapping or squalling and always dirty. As far as Hanani could tell, Hoshea did nothing to aid her in any way or to discipline their brood.

"By the grace of Elohim, if I ever have children, they will not act like this bunch!" mumbled Hanani. "I will see to their discipline. Not that I will ever have any, banished away as I am in this desert hole!"

To his detachment Hoshea never complained, but countered complaints with positive words.

"Warriors," he would ask, "did you enjoy your long night's sleep on your soft downy mats? And how about your wonderful morning meal? I think this fortress is the finest in all Israel, agreed?"

"How does he do it?" Hanani asked the other guards. "I see nothing here of any value to praise."

"Well, think about it," answered his buddy Joab. "There are some palms and a jujube tree by the spring. Just look at that scrawny acacia out there! In the distance is a tiny oasis with some palm trees. And those hills! Aren't they attractive in their dirty brown dress? Man, there's life here! Once in awhile we can see jackals, wolves, hyenas, rabbits, serpents and even scorpions. I hear we have lions, but I haven't spotted one yet. Finally, on the plus side, you have this grubby bunch of companions. What more could you possibly want?"

"What more could I want? Are you kidding me? We have some decrepit walls and gates to guard, a few scraggly goats to tend and an occasional march to the hills. Other than that," he added in miserable tones, "what's to praise? We have no female companionship. We have nothing to eat but flat cakes, goat curds, dates, a few vegetables that we can coax out of this sand and a tiny ration of wine. O Elohim, why have you left us here at the end of the earth? Except for Sabbath rest and games we can play under our flickering oil lamps, it's always the same—boring, boring, boring!"

The only relief was an occasional caravan passing through toward Egypt or from Arabia to points north. Then, during its overnight stop, things were noisy. The caravan drovers were a smelly, scraggly-bearded and hard-bitten bunch from who knew what people. They bristled with dangerous-looking curved swords and handmade knives. Their garb was a strange mixture of tunics and robes the worse for wear and badly needing a washing. They sported turbans of once-bright colors. They got roaring drunk and recounted tales that stretched the imagination beyond all reason. Their humor was coarse and obscene, but at least it gave the troopers something to laugh about.

"Say, you green little warriors," their leader sneered, "let me tell you about the women in far-off India. They dress only in skimpy transparent gowns. Can they ever dance! And that's not all they can do. You haven't been loved until you've been loved by one of those wild creatures!"

And so on and on it went into the night, until finally the commander appeared and put a stop to it.

"Warriors, to your posts! Those of you not on duty get to your mats! Morning will soon be on us. You caravaners, get some rest. I'm running you out of here at dawn."

"Who do you think you are, commander?" their leader angrily retorted. "We take no orders from you or any other man!"

"Oh? While you are in my fortress, you will take orders from me, for I am the law here. Shall I prove it?"

"Alright, high-and-mighty Law. We will be off tomorrow, but we're never coming back to this miserable place!"

"That is fine with me. The only thing I will want to see of you in the morning is the dust you kick up as you leave."

"Man," grumbled Hanani. "He is tough! If we had any silver, we could buy something from the caravaners, but we don't have a piece of silver to our name. Our Great King Solomon has forgotten all about us. Hey, Eliphaz, how long has it been since we received any pay, rations or fresh clothing?"

"I don't know, but Commander Hoshea does. Commander," he shouted, "when did we last receive any pay or provisions?"

"Why do you want to know? Do you want to register a complaint? It is not for you to question such matters. In good time we will receive our allotments."

Hanani grunted unhappily, "Of course—in good time!"

"Warrior, aren't you forgetting something? First, you are not to answer your commander sarcastically. And second, you are already past due on the wall. Now get on with your watch!"

Tamar

With that Hanani buckled on his sword, picked up his shield and spear, shuffled up the stairs and again started his interminable rounds—100 steps west, 100 steps south... He almost longed to see an enemy approaching. At least, that would be a diversion from their forced exile.

They did have one welcome diversion, however. It seldom rained in the Negev, but one morning the entire fortress was suddenly drenched by a serious storm. The warriors all ran out and danced around in it, whooping like little children.

But the rain was gone as suddenly as it came and the desert sand soaked it up as rapidly as it had fallen. But then, a surprise awaited the fortress contingent. Days later, seeds lying dormant in the ground sprang up and blossomed into the most beautiful flowers imaginable. The desert literally blossomed like a rose, a sight the warriors would not soon forget. The desolate desert had its glorious side, as Elohim painted it from his many-hued palette of yellow, orange, pink, red, blue and purple.

Another diversion they seldom acknowledged was the wonder Adonai revealed each night in the crystal-clear sky of the high desert—His awe-inspiring expanse high overhead. Thousands of stars gleamed like pinpoints of light pricked through the blackness of the canopy above them, to allow heavenly light to shine through. Once in awhile during his night watch Hanani would murmur David's psalm, *"Declareth the Heavens the glory of God, showeth His handiwork the firmament."*

During the tranquil blackness of the night, Hanani was temporarily at peace with his world and his fortress. Nothing seemed to bring any dramatic change to his life as a warrior at Tamar. At the end of his conscription period, he might even leave the place reluctantly. Then suddenly came a change to his life...

scroll 4

Time to Command . . . Sort of

"Caravan, ho!" shouted a lookout one sparkling day. "It is one of ours." Hoshea soon appeared on the wall, watching it lumber toward the gates. Praise Elohim, finally a commission from the Great King had arrived!

Once the caravan had entered the fortress and its leader reported to Hoshea, he announced to his troopers that they had received new orders, back pay and provisions. Finally the outpost had real food—fresh fruit all the way from Damascus, melons, wheat, dates, figs, and a new stock of wine. What a relief from the poor fare they had been eating!

"Tonight we celebrate with a feast," Hoshea announced to his cheering warriors.

Even though they had nothing on which to spend it, the warriors' back pay was more than welcome. Suddenly they were richer than they had ever been. They had a handful of real silver—odd-shaped little bits of silver, but they could be used to barter for something . . . anything.

"What are you going to do with your sudden wealth?" Joab asked Hanani.

"Don't know. I guess I will save it up. Some day I hope to marry the most beautiful girl in the world. My only hope is to attract her with my 'wealth.'"

"That's quite a dream. At your pay you will have to save up for about a hundred years."

"Well, I have to start somewhere."

Tamar

At the end of their "banquet" the commander called for the attention of his chattering guards.

"Form a file and count off, one, two, one, two, one, two." All of the ones to the left and all of the twos to the right."

They were soon divided into two equal groups plus one.

"Now, the number ones will prepare to accompany me and my household to Ezion-geber, where you will be stationed at the king's royal docks. Our task will be to protect his merchant ships and crews from pirates while they are in port and to guard the city from raiders. All of the number twos will remain at our garrison. Who is the odd man in this group? You, Hanani! You will serve as the interim commander here until a replacement arrives very shortly with fresh troops. Since you are literate, you can make up rosters and keep records. The rest of you will obey Hanani's orders until he is relieved of his command. Understood?"

"Yes, Sir!" the left-behind force answered despondently.

"Dismissed, then. Hanani, you will make up a duty roster that will serve until reinforcements arrive. I realize that your numbers will be few, but spread the duty around as best you can. Show me the list before I leave."

"I will do that, Sir. May I say that you have been an excellent commander? I, for one, am sorry to see you leave."

"Thank you, Hanani," he answered in the din of a rousing shout from the entire contingent. As he returned to his mat, Hanani thought what a great assignment Ezion-geber would be—the beautiful sea, the bustling port, the Great King's fleet bringing exotic plants and animals, gold, silver and jewels from far places, cool ocean breezes . . .

"Oh, well," he muttered. "That isn't what I ended up with, so I will just have to do the best I can with what has been dealt to me."

There was little sleep that night. Those departing were busy loading up the commander's household furnishings and supplies on a crude wagon to be pulled by one of the outpost's mules.

"No, no!" Hoshea's wife shrieked at the warriors. "Don't put my good pots at the bottom of the load. Watch what you are doing! I don't want a single scratch on my furniture. Children, quit running around like wild animals! You can help by either staying out of the way or by carrying small items to the wagon."

Her orders were largely ignored, as the departees laughed and shouted. Of course, the children continued to noisily romp, adding to the din and dust billowing up on everyone.

Time to Command . . . Sort of

It was barely dawn the next morning when Hoshea summoned his appointed contingent, saw that they were ready and ordered them to march out.

"Well, we are now a minimal force, but must make the most of our situation. I will assign duties to each of us. Be extra vigilant, because some enemy may find out about our weakness and take advantage of it."

Some grumbled that they had drawn night duty, but Hanani told them that all, including him, would share equally in both night and day duty.

One evening three strangers arrived at the gate and asked permission to enter. The code of hospitality practiced far and wide meant that they were to be admitted and offered food and lodging for the night. Hanani asked them,

"Honored guests, who are you and from where do you come?"

"We are Midianites, escaping the wrath of our clan chief. Please grant us asylum."

"Very well, you may remain here for three days, but must then continue your flight. We have few provisions to share."

"Thank you, kind commander. We promise to abide by your wishes."

Hanani had no idea that the three were really spies, to search out their weaknesses.

"Did you notice how few they are in numbers?" one of the three whispered to the others. "They also have limited resources, according to the statement about their supply of food. This fortress will be child's play to take down."

The three caused Hanani no trouble, but observed every detail, even the guard duty rotation. On the morning of the fourth day, they bade farewell to their hosts and left. However, one of the soldiers on guard duty noticed that they returned toward Midian. He thought this a strange direction for fugitives from there to take, so called down to Hanani to join him. When he pointed out the direction in which the three went, Hanani told him,

"A good observation and I agree with you that this doesn't look right. We must redouble our vigilance. Soon we may have many more guests, this time uninvited."

Several nights later, guards on the walls heard muffled sounds from outside the walls. One quietly descended to alert Hanani. He called out his entire force, had them hurriedly arm in the dark and placed them along the walls. He instructed them,

Tamar

"Have plenty of arrows and also stones for your slings. I'm ordering our cook to prepare large pots of boiling oil, to 'anoint' our guests. If this is an enemy force and if it attacks at a certain point at the gates or along the walls, I will signal most of you to that point."

scroll 5

First Brush with Danger

As darkness gave way to dawn, the guards could see a sizeable party of what appeared to be Midianites armed to the teeth. There must have been 200 of them. They were carrying ladders to use in scaling the walls.

"Bring them on," whispered Hanani. "We are ready to welcome them."

With that he raised his arm and the entire contingent gave a loud shout. The nearest Midianites were treated to a shower of arrows and then a hailstorm of stones, slung with deadly accuracy. A fourth of the enemy lay on the ground, either dead or badly wounded. The remaining enemy hurled blasphemies at the defendants and then retreated, only to circle around and try another part of the wall. Again they were repulsed, with many more of them down. Finally, they made an assault on the gates, attempting to set them afire with blazing arrows.

"Quickly!" shouted Hanani, "bring water and dowse those arrows! And while you are about it, toss some jars of oil out onto the entrance ramp. We'll fight fire with fire. Wrap some arrows with old rags, soak them in oil and shoot them onto the ramp. The oil should ignite and discourage them from trying a frontal assault. But be careful to throw the jars far enough out that no oil is splattered back toward the gates."

While this was going on, a few of the Midianites separated themselves from the main force and succeeded in mounting a ladder. Over the wall they came, shouting their murderous war cries. Hanani ordered his best archers, "Turn and take them out!" The intruders only made a few running steps before they were downed.

Hanani calculated that the Midianites had lost half of their number, with no losses among the defenders. One had caught an arrow in his shoulder and another had burned his hand with boiling oil, but otherwise, they were safe and sound.

The Midianites must have counted their losses, also, because just as quickly as they had arrived, they left, running toward their camels staked out some distance from the fortress.

"All of you did heroic service," Hanani told his warriors. "I'm proud of you. However, we need to keep a sharp lookout. They will be back, in even larger numbers and thirsty for revenge. Meanwhile, we need to strip the dead of their weapons and then give them a proper burial. We will carry them to a cave in yonder hills and place them in it. Then we will seal the cave as best we can. All except those on guard duty take a wagon and load up the bodies."

This unsavory task was eventually accomplished, and close to a hundred enemy warriors were laid like logs in a cave. It was then sealed with large stones. The only positive result, other than repulsing the Midianites, was a large number of weapons, items of clothing, metal wristbands and even some small pieces of gold and silver they confiscated.

Things went along normally over the next few days. Then late one afternoon the lookout shouted,

"Warriors arriving from the west. They appear to be ours."

"Gate guards," Hanani ordered, "when we are certain they are our people, open the gates to them."

"They are our reinforcements," shouted down the sentinel. "I can count 36 warriors, plus their commander and a woman with him. There are three wagons with drivers and servants."

"Praise Elohim, our reinforcements have finally arrived! Our skeleton force will be back up to full strength," Hanani shouted to his men.

The new troops entered the fortress, tired, thirsty and dust-covered. Hanani presented himself as interim commander to the new commander, Ba'ana, who ordered all of his warriors to stand at attention while he introduced both himself and his conscripts, then asked Hanani to introduce his little squad. With that formality over, Ba'ana presented his mother, Abigail.

First Brush with Danger

"She needs a home and I am a widower, so I take her with me to act as my cook and housekeeper, as well as a source of love and comfort."

"It is a great honor to meet you, mother of Ba'ana," Hanani answered for his troopers. "You will inherit more than 50 sons while you are here. Whatever we can do to help you, please ask us."

"Thank you, my son."

Once the new men had been dismissed to the barracks to stow their gear and rest briefly before the evening meal, Ba'ana turned to the supply wagons they had brought and ordered the drivers and their helpers to unhitch the mules and provide water and forage for them. He added,

"Then we will empty the wagons and store the supplies we brought. I imagine the men here could use a bit of variety in diet. I know they will be happy to receive a change of undergarments and tunics, as well as silver for their purses."

"Yes, Sir," Hanani responded enthusiastically.

"Now, Hanani, bring me up to date on happenings here."

"Well, Sir, the only matter of any importance was an attack by about 200 Midianites. Our men were capable and courageous. I commend them highly to you. We repulsed the enemy with arrows, slings and boiling oil. Only two of our men were wounded and none killed, while we brought to an inglorious end about half of the Midianites' number. I suspect they will be back with an even larger force, bloodthirsty for revenge."

"Excellent! I think you are right about those accursed Midianites. We will keep a vigilant watch for them and will have a surprise in store for them when they do come. I will demonstrate it to the men tomorrow. I would like for you to continue as my adjutant, caring for the roster and other duties I will assign to you. Is that acceptable?"

"Yes, Sir!"

The next morning Ba'ana called his entire force together and ordered the cover to be removed from a mysterious object on one of the wagons.

"This, warriors," he explained, "is a sling of tremendous power. It can hurl a stone the size of your head 500 paces or more. Six men are required to operate its pulleys and ratchets. I guarantee the Midianites or anyone else will think twice about attacking us after they get a taste of this weapon."

"Amazing, Sir!" spoke up Hanani. "Will you teach us how to use it?"

"Certainly, beginning now."

After a few days of practice, the entire troop had become skilled at operating the monster sling. They had practiced on some rock outcroppings a distance away and had shattered them. Now all they lacked were some enemy bodies at which to aim.

The only difficulties Hanani encountered and reported were some small friction between the older and newer groups of warriors. He also mentioned the griping going on among the recent arrivals. Ba'ana responded that he would expect nothing less from them. Then Hanani brought up the fact that one newcomer had been sleeping at his post during night duty.

"Well, the first problem is normal," Ba'ana commented. "It will take time for the new contingent to adjust to life here. The second is problematic. What is the name of your drowsy guard?"

"Pallu."

"Is he on duty tonight?"

"Yes, Sir, on the second watch."

"I will take a quiet walk around and see if I can catch him."

Just as Hanani had reported, Pallu had fallen asleep at his post. Ba'ana waited until morning and then called out his entire company.

"Warriors, something dangerous has been going on here. Pallu has been asleep at his post."

"I?" asked Pallu indignantly. "Who told you that?"

"I made the rounds during your watch and found you asleep. Since you put the entire fortress in danger, you must be punished—forty lashes, minus one, and then confined to the barracks for seven days on bread and water."

"No! I will never do that again. Just give me another chance."

"You will have another chance, but only after receiving your punishment. Hanani, bind him to the whipping post. Since I ordered the lashes, I will administer them. The entire company will sound off the lashes and make sure you count them correctly."

Ba'ana brought out a whip and began the scourging. "One! Two! Three . . . !" on the bleeding back of the culprit, as he moaned in agony . . . and on to thirty-nine, each lash shouted out by the entire troop. Then Pallu was led into the barracks, where the commander personally anointed his back with a healing salve. He then lay down on his stomach, the only position that didn't hurt, and fell into a fitful sleep.

"Let the crime and punishment be recorded," Ba'ana announced to the still-assembled troops. "I do not enjoy meting out punishment, but when it must be done, I will see to it. Learn a lesson from this: None of us is exempt

First Brush with Danger

from being punished for wrongdoing, and none is overlooked for praise, when it is called for. Now, dismissed for your morning meal. Afterward, you will pick up your duties as usual."

The lesson was burned into their hearts. No one dared drowse off while on duty, nor willingly disobeyed any other regulations. They knew that their commander was just, as well as kind. After his confinement, Pallu returned to the roster, chastened and remorseful.

Things were quiet at Tamar—too quiet! Then one day it happened! An ominous-looking cloud appeared in the east—a cyclonic sandstorm. Lookouts warned the command of impending danger.

scroll 6

Mother of All Sandstorms

"Attention in the fortress! A monster sandstorm is bearing down on us!"

Ba'ana ran out into the courtyard, shouting,

"Bring in the mules and goats! Bar the gates and windows. Close the cooking area. Everyone wet down your headpiece and cover your face, to protect your eyes, nose and mouth. Turn away from the wind and position yourselves along the east wall. You, Hanani, run get my mother!"

They had hardly completed these assignments when the gale struck with savage force, filling the courtyard with a span or more of fine sand. It howled its way through the fortress and just as rapidly as it came, it moved on westward.

"Everyone safe?" asked the commander. "Sound off one by one!"

Soon the garrison was accounted for and the task began of removing the sand from inside the fortress. It had gotten into almost everything, so a general cleanup was called for. Ba'ana asked his mother to take charge of the sweeping and wiping off, a task she happily accepted. She made a quick circuit and shouted,

"Here, warriors! This is not good enough! Take your sleeping mats outside and shake them thoroughly. Do the same with your spare clothing. Then sweep up this floor. What? You say you already did? Not by my standards, you didn't! Do it again!"

Finally she found everything to be pretty much rid of sand. She thanked the troops and returned to her house to clean it up. Several warriors volunteered to help her. Soon the house, too, was clean.

Mother of All Sandstorms

This sandstorm episode only generated a lot more complaining about living conditions at Tamar.

"This has to be the worst place on earth!" spouted one trooper. "You would think we were sent here as punishment."

"Brother, I agree," chimed in another warrior. "The sooner we can get out of here the better! My little village and home up north never looked better. I didn't think so before, but I do now."

Hanani finally spoke up.

"Look, we are here, so we might as well accept it. We can learn some lessons about endurance. We have discovered that life back home was pretty good, after all. Now we need to learn to patiently accept our life here."

The garrison turned quiet as it pondered his words. Back home was good! When they returned there, they would value it much more then they had before. Meanwhile, they would face life at Tamar with more patience and courage. The latter they would soon need.

scroll 7

Captured!

EARLY ONE MORNING THE commander called Hanani to choose a partner and go out on a hunting expedition. They had had no meat for some time and he didn't want to kill one of the goats.

"Find what you can of kosher animals," he instructed Hanani. "An Oryx would be good, or an ibex, or even some doves."

"Yes, Sir!" Hanani happily answered. "I choose Joel to go with me. He is an excellent marksman."

"Very good. Be back by sunset, however, and may Elohim direct your arrows!"

The two set out in high spirits. This would be a wonderful break from routine. They headed toward the distant mountains and a little oasis near them. That should be an ideal place to find game. They stealthily approached the oasis, hoping to take some animal by surprise. Little did they know, however, that they were the game. They had been stalked for some distance by a party of Edomites who saw a golden opportunity to capture and hold two enemy warriors for ransom.

The Edomites circled silently around Hanani and Joel and waited until the two had located a small herd of ibex, with one majestic male, his horns curving back over his hindquarters. They inched their way closer and closer, and then shot down the ibex. The others scattered and, in the confusion, the Edomites struck, clubbing the two before they could mount a defense. Loading their unconscious bodies, along with the ibex, onto horses, the raiding party headed back to their land east of Tamar.

When the two regained consciousness, they were permitted to sit on the horses, but remained securely bound. They tried to reason with their captors, but got nowhere.

"Look," Hanani pled with them, "Let us go and you will be rewarded by our commander. If you do not release us, rest assured that he will bring a large force to rescue us."

The Edomites merely laughed at them.

"Oh, and just how will he do that?" their chief asked. "There is no way in which he can penetrate our stronghold."

"He will find a way, mark what I am saying."

"Yes, of course he will find a way. Has he suddenly become your god, because only a god can enter our fortress without permission."

When night came on, the raiders stopped at Ir-nahash, tying their hostages to tamarisks. They were given a crust of bread and some water and then left securely bound for the night.

The next morning, when Hanani and Joel still failed to show up, Ba'ana ordered trackers to find out what had happened to them. One of the guards told him that the two had headed toward the hills. Six well-armed trackers were sent out in search of them. Following their footprints, the searchers discovered a confusing pattern of other footprints and then horse tracks. It was obvious that Hanani and Joel had been abducted.

"Sir," they reported back to Ba'ana, "it appears that our men have been captured and taken eastward. Our best count indicates twelve or so horses in the raiding party. We thought it best to report this to you first, and then follow their trail. Do you wish to lead us?"

"Thank you for your diligence," Ba'ana answered. "We will take a small party out immediately in pursuit of them. You trackers will guide us. Be prepared to leave very soon. You, Yohanan, will be responsible for the fortress while we are gone."

In short order twelve of their own number, plus Ba'ana, had packed up simple provisions and extra weapons. They were soon on their way, in pursuit of the abductors. Not having horses, their way was somewhat slow. They stopped for the night in a shallow cave and early the next morning were again on their mission.

"Sir," shouted an advance tracker, "here is where they passed the night. Judging by depressions in the sand, their captives were tied up to trees. This means they are still alive."

"Good work! Anything else that might give us a clue as to the identity of the kidnappers?"

Another tracker reported finding a broken pot by a campfire. He examined it and said, "It has the style and markings of Edomite ware."

"So! If they are Edomites, they may be heading to their stronghold at Sela. Let us assume that for now and continue eastward, tracking them as best we can."

Their pursuit led them down into the hot, forbidding Arabáh. For the most part it was flat and arid, well below sea level—no place in which to tarry. Only some colorful cliffs and buttes in the distance broke its monotony. They crossed it in the devilish heat of the day, perspiring profusely. They stopped for the night in a small cave on the desolate uphill slopes that led to the Eastern Highlands. Just as dawn was breaking, they resumed their quest, but with greater caution. The raiding party was still ahead of them, but they could not determine exactly how far ahead. After a steady climb, evening was fast approaching, with welcome relief from the stifling heat. Suddenly they came upon a gorge in the rocky mountains, so narrow that one could extend his arms and touch, in places, both walls.

"I have heard of this place," Ba'ana said. "It is a pass leading to Sela itself. We don't dare enter it this late in the evening, because even during the day, it is dark and forbidding. We will back off and seek shelter for the night in a well-hidden place. In the morning we will decide whether to penetrate it or find another way into the citadel."

While this was going on, Hanani and Joel were already in Sela. They had shuddered at the length, darkness and narrowness of the pass, thinking that only a handful of defenders in that cleft could hold off an army. Because

Captured!

of the angle of the gorge's steep walls, little to no sunlight filtered into it. One had the feeling that he was in a tortuous high tunnel, with only a very occasional glimpse of sky.

Finally the party came out of the cleft and into intense sunlight. The stronghold itself was almost as forbidding as the pass. They couldn't help but notice that steep and treacherous cliffs surrounded the place. Carved out of their red rock surface was a series of structures. This was amazing to the prisoners.

"What an ordeal it must have been to chisel out all of these buildings," Hanani commented. Despite being a captive, he was alert to every detail of the place. He murmured to Joel,

"There appears to be no good way in except through the canyon, since high cliffs surround them. How can we ever be rescued, even if an entire army shows up?"

They were being escorted, still trussed up, along the single long street that was Sela. To their surprise, they saw no women or children; only men, most of them in military service. Obviously, this was not a city, but a citadel.

Finally, they were taken down roughly from their horses and dragged unceremoniously into a military headquarters, carved, as everything in Sela, out of the rusty-red walls of the canyon.

"So, Israelite pigs!" the headquarters commander spat out at them. "We thank you for the excellent ibex you killed for us. In payment, you will be held for a handsome ransom. If it is not paid, you will become our slaves."

"You will regret this," Hanani said. "Our warriors will hunt you down and you will die at their hands."

"Brave talk for a prisoner! You have been through our entrance gorge. Just how do you suppose your warriors can subdue us in that narrow channel?"

"They will find a way, I can assure you," Hanani answered.

"Enough! Guards, take these prisoners to the inner cell and shackle them there."

"Yes, commander," they answered as they dragged the two off to their new prison home."

Once alone in the dark, clammy cave that served as a prison, and chained tightly to posts, the two pondered how they could possibly escape the clutches of the Edomites. They were positive that Ba'ana and his garrison would not allow this to pass unchallenged. Yet it would take a much larger force than they had available to penetrate into the stronghold itself.

And could their commander actually piece together what had happened to them and who had done it?

Ba'ana and his scouting force hid away for the night beneath a rocky ledge not far from the pass. Early the next morning he took another look at the narrow entrance channel and decided that they could not safely enter it unchallenged. What could they do? Was there another way in? He sent two scouts to climb the high cliffs before them and see if they could spot another approach. They returned in a few hours to report that any other approach would be extremely steep. They had seen that descending those cliffs into the stronghold during daylight hours would make them highly visible from below. Yet, how could they possibly manage to descend those treacherous slopes at night?

Ba'ana decided that the only recourse was to request a force of warriors to storm not only the gorge, but to descend into the stronghold from many different points simultaneously. Could they use their ancestor Gideon's ruse and attack at night? Perhaps the enemy could be fooled into thinking that thousands of warriors were attacking them, rather than a relative handful.

Accomplishing this would only require a few hundred warriors, which perhaps could be called out from fortresses throughout the Negev and as far north as Jerusalem. He wrote a scroll to the garrison commanders, outlining his plan and requesting their immediate aid. A runner was selected to take this scroll to Tamar. From there other runners would carry copies to the different fortresses, including the headquarters garrison in the capital. This was his message:

> Ba'ana, commander of the king's fortress at Tamar, to all fellow commanders at garrisons in the Negev and the Capital. Two or our best warriors have been captured by what appear to be Edomite raiders. They have been taken to Sela, where we are certain they are held as prisoners. I humbly request as many warriors as you can spare to join my small force just outside of the gorge leading to Sela. Since the stronghold is surrounded by high cliffs, I propose to use Gideon's strategy—attack at night with shofars and torches, confusing the enemy warriors into thinking that we have them surrounded. Please bring shofars and pitchers. Torches will

Captured!

be provided. I anticipate your cooperation and will be watching in a stronghold of our own for the arrival of your forces. I think you will agree that two of our brave warriors are worth more than a thousand of the Edomite dogs. May the strong arm of El Shaddai bring your warriors safely to us.

All Ba'ana and his men could do now was to wait. They had to find food, so he sent out warriors by twos to bring down game. Fortunately, they had located a small spring near their hideout, so water was no problem. Quail were all they could bag, so these would have to suffice.

Ba'ana calculated that his runner would have reached Tamar in two days. Copies of his message would take a little time to transcribe, but by the morning of the third day other runners should be on their way.

"Let's see," he mused, "fortresses at Beersheba, Araor, Avdat, Arad, Ziklag and Debir should take a runner at least four days to reach. If warriors started from each of those fortresses by the next day, they should arrive at Tamar within five days and then on here within another two days. That is almost two weeks, if all that goes smoothly and rapidly. A long time, but it cannot be helped. I pray to Elohim that my two warriors survive."

The commander at Sela lost no time in having a scroll sent to the Great King Solomon himself, demanding an exorbitant ransom for his two warriors.

"He is so rich," the commander said to himself, "he cannot even count his wealth. What are ten thousand shekels in gold to him?"

Runners carried the scroll, under diplomatic immunity, to Jerusalem. Stopped at a gate, they presented their official document to the captain of the guard. He read it and took it immediately to the palace, where it was presented to the king himself. He ordered the couriers into his presence and commented,

"This is a high price for just two men. How do I know you have them?"

"Here, Sire," one of them answered, "is the private signet of each."

"You run a perilous course, doubly so because you are related to us through our ancestors Abraham and Isaac. Where is your country's sense of common blood? Where is your sense of community and mutual support with us? If you refuse to honor our relationship, you will be cut off permanently. Transmit this to your rulers. I will take this matter up with my advisors and military commanders. Meanwhile, you will be my guests, under guard, here in the palace. I hope you will be comfortable. But remember that my hospitality has its limits. Any efforts to abuse your stay here will be dealt with properly. In such an eventuality, where shall we send your heads?"

"Sire, you can expect nothing but our best behavior while here."

"I pray so. Now you are dismissed. Commander, take them to the guest quarters and assign guards day and night to them."

"Yes, Sire!"

While the king was conferring with his counsel, the scroll from Ba'ana arrived. It was read in his presence. He chuckled at the strategy planned by Ba'ana and asked the garrison commander to send a detachment to his aid.

"I would enjoy being there to watch that nighttime show!" the king commented. "Let us stall the messengers from Sela on the pretext that we are conferring with our fortress commanders in the south."

The next day a troop of sturdy warriors, all capable of running great distances, was sent off from the capital at a trot. Meanwhile, warriors from other fortresses were on the way to their target. The pieces were falling into place. When all was ready, a surprise would be in store for the "impregnable" stronghold at Sela.

scroll 8

Sela Has Unexpected Guests

JUST AS BA'ANA HAD calculated almost to the day, troops began approaching Sela. His lookouts spotted them and sent word down to direct them to his temporary stronghold. One by one they arrived hot and tired, but eager to get on with the task before them. To Ba'ana's elation, a force from Jerusalem also arrived and reported in. Ba'ana counted them all up and found that he had some 250 warriors, the pick of each garrison, at his disposal. All of them had shofars and pitchers, as his instructions had stated. Torches had been prepared for them from dead wood scattered about beneath the few trees in the area.

Ba'ana addressed his assembled garrisons:

"Fellow warriors, I wish to thank you and your commanders for coming to our aid. Sela is a most difficult place to penetrate. We cannot succeed by entering through its very confining gorge. We must enter the stronghold from the mountains surrounding it. Here is my plan: We will climb the mountains at many points during the night, a difficult task. We will hide out around the citadel all day until darkness settles in. Then, following Gideon's successful strategy, we will place our lighted torches in our pitchers. Then I will blow my shofar and brandish my burning torch. All of you do the same, shouting, 'For El Shaddai!' We will descend as rapidly as possible, continuing to shout and wave torches. That should confuse the garrison there into thinking that we are thousands, not hundreds. Understood?"

"Yes, Sir!" the combined force answered in unison. Several added, "This should be great fun!"

The Edomite commander went to the cell where Hanani and Joel remained shackled. Laughing at their plight, he announced,

"Helpless circumcised pigs, you have little manhood left. When I am through with you, you will have none left. Then, you will be eunuchs for life, bowing and scraping before me. I have sent a message to your king demanding ten thousand shekels' weight in gold for your release. Until now I have received no answer, nor have my emissaries returned. We will wait a few more days, and if there is no response or a negative response, I will have great pleasure in taking a knife to you and turning you into meek little slaves."

"You will regret this action," Hanani answered. "Our great God will bring you down!"

"Oh? And why hasn't he done so? Can it be that he is a god only of your little country and has no power in our great land? What can he possibly do to reach our impregnable stronghold?"

"You will see. No one speaks ill of Elohim and survives for long."

The commander spat on the cell floor and exclaimed,

"So much for your miserable god and your weak-kneed people!"

With that he strode out, laughing obscenely.

The trap was set. Soldiers surrounded the stronghold, hiding out until dark. The sun went down and the night crept in on silent wings. All awaited Ba'ana's signal. They prayed and shifted from one leg to another, shofar in one hand and a torch in the other, hidden inside a pitcher.

When Ba'ana finally blew the signal and lifted his torch, the canyon below him echoed from the hundreds of shouts and blasts on shofars. The troops then descended as rapidly as they could on the steep, rocky terrain. When they reached level ground, they pursued the Edomites, who, in their confusion, were attempting to escape. Some ran into the gorge, but Ba'ana had left a detachment there to block their escape. Others ran toward the far end of the valley in which Sela was located. Reaching there, they found

Sela Has Unexpected Guests

the enemy everywhere, firing volleys of arrows and stones. Many of the Edomites died. Soon those still living were captured and disarmed.

Then Ba'ana and his own warriors went in search of their two captured colleagues. Ba'ana confronted several cowering Edomites.

"Where are your two captives?" he barked. "Tell me now or one moment from now you will be dead!"

With this death threat hanging over them, they gave Ba'ana the location of the prison. He and his Tamar group were soon in the garrison headquarters and came face to face with the enemy commander and two of his guards.

"So you thought you could get away with capturing two of our men and defying Elohim, did you? Lay down your weapons. Your entire force has been killed or captured, so it is no use resisting further."

"Go to Sheol!" was the commander's venomous answer, refusing to disarm himself.

"Go there yourself!"

With that Ba'ana threw his lance, pinning the commander to a wall. His two guards quickly dropped their weapons and surrendered.

"Now, where are your prisoners?"

No answer was forthcoming, so Ba'ana had them trussed up and drew his sword.

"Again, where are the prisoners?"

"Don't kill us. They're in the inner cell, that way."

Ba'ana raced to the inner cell and found his two comrades well shackled but surprised and overjoyed at seeing him.

"How did you get in here?" Hanani asked.

"I will explain shortly. First, we will free you. Guards, in here now!"

The two guards were pushed into the cell and ordered to unshackle the two prisoners. They claimed,

"We don't remember how!"

"Oh? Perhaps I can convince you to remember. I will start chopping off your fingers, one by one, until your failed memory is restored."

"No, please! The key is in the commander's quarters, hanging on the wall."

"Two of you men run and get it," he ordered.

Two of his warriors returned in short order. Finally, he was able to release the prisoners' shackles and led them out of the building. They were so stiff that he and his troops had to help them walk. Once outside, they

45

Tamar

rejoined their comrades and their many other fellow warriors. A great cheer went up as they arrived, still walking slowly.

"Sir," Hanani asked, "how did you manage to put together all of these warriors?"

"We sent runners to the other garrisons, even to the one in Jerusalem. The response was very gratifying. Sound off, warriors from the different garrisons."

"Jerusalem!"
"Beersheba!"
"Arad!"
"Araor!"
"Ziklag!"
"Debir!"
"Avdat!"

"Wonderful! But this is still a modest 'army.' How did you manage to get through the gorge and enter the stronghold?"

"Have you ever heard the story of Gideon?"

"Of course . . . Oh, now I understand the significance of the shofars we heard. You used his strategy to confuse and frighten the enemy."

"Yes, and it worked just as well now as it did for Gideon. Our mighty Lord has again done a glorious work on our behalf. Most of the garrison is dead and the remaining defenders have surrendered."

"What a story to tell our children and grandchildren!" Joel said.

"Now, load up with provisions from the storage rooms here and all of the weapons you can find. I saw some wagons and mules. Let us put them to good use. It is time to return to our garrisons. But first, let us all bow in prayer:

> Great Lord Elohim, creator of the heavens and the earth, and sustainer of your people, we give you the honor and praise for your intervention this day on our behalf. As you have guided and protected us on our quest, now guide us safely back to our fortresses. Allelu-ya. Amen.

Ba'ana personally clasped the hand and shoulder of every soldier present, again thanked all of them and sent them on their way under Elohim's protective hand. They all shouted "Shalom!" as each left with choice Edomite weapons, clothing, food and a handful of confiscated gold and silver. Then Ba'ana and his contingent headed out through the gorge and on their way "home," loaded down with loot. They took their time, sighting the fortress on the third day.

But a terrible shock awaited them! To their horror they discovered the entrance doors burnt and the fortress sacked. Some of their colleagues were dead and others missing. Ba'ana raced to his home to find it ransacked and his mother dead. Anguished, he cried,

"Why, Lord? Why did you permit this? Who is responsible? They must be made to pay severely."

scroll 9
Ba'ana's Revenge

BA'ANA MOURNED OPENLY BEFORE his small band, not just for his mother, but for their fallen comrades, as well. When he finally composed himself, he said,

"We must determine the culprits. See if you can find arrows or other items that might give us a clue to their identity. But first, we have the solemn duty to bury my beloved mother and our fallen warriors."

He chose a cave in the mountain range and, with tender hands, wrapped the body of his mother in her best robe. He then placed her remains on a natural shelf in the cave. The fallen warriors were dressed in their parade uniforms and also deposited in the cave. After a tearful prayer on their behalf, he ordered the cave sealed with a mound of large stones. After about an hour of hard physical labor, the solemn task was finished and the warriors slowly returned to their destroyed fortress. Once there, he sent scouts out to determine the identity of this unknown enemy and the size of their force.

"Sir," one of the warriors said upon his return, "here are some arrows that have the marks of Midianite workmanship."

"And I found a pouch containing a Midianite seal," spoke up another warrior.

"That makes it plain. The Modalities may have observed us leaving for Sela and took advantage of our absence. They appear to have had a large force. Let us examine the area, to see if we can find any tracks, human or camel."

Ba'ana's Revenge

They soon found myriads of tracks, including those of apparently hundreds of camels.

"So it was a large force, indeed! We will rest overnight and then go in pursuit of them. We are so few that we will have to devise another unusual strategy, if we are to defeat them and free their captives. Dismissed!"

Right after a hurried meal the next dawn, Ba'ana and twelve warriors, including Hanani and Joab, hurried south, following the camel tracks. The trail led them for eight days to the eastern arm of the Red Sea. On the way they hurried through a barren and inhospitable desert. Black volcanic mountains arose abruptly out of the harsh and rocky desert floor, dwarfing nearby dusty ochre cliffs.

"This is no place for man or beast!" Hanani observed to Ba'ana. "And to think that Moses had to lead our ancestors around in this fearful region!"

"Without water," Ba'ana answered, "we wouldn't survive here long."

Reaching the sea, Ba'ana gave his men a short respite. Shedding their sandals, they splashed in its azure waters. Returning to their hike, they skirted the sea to the right, entering the border of Midian, a semi-barren land broken up by two north-south ranges of mountains.

As they approached Midian, Ba'ana revealed his attack plan to his tiny force.

"We will use bandit tactics, placing ourselves in a circle around the enemy camp during the night. Then just before dawn we will shoot flaming arrows into their tents. As they run out, we will attack them. Then we will fade into the desert and be well hidden before it is fully light. To cover our tracks, we will sweep them away behind us with palm fronds. On a later night we will attack right after they have bedded down, first dispatching their guards. We will again melt into the landscape. And we will untie their camels, spook them and send them galloping away. Any questions? No? Then let us prepare for our first night of entertainment."

An advance scout reported to Ba'ana that a large Midianite camp was just ahead, located by an oasis.

"I saw no women or children," he observed, "so it must be our target band. Many camels are staked out nearby. There are low hills surrounding the oasis. It is ideal for your plan, Sir. We can place ourselves around the camp and be ready for our surprise attack."

"Good work! Warriors, let us hide out until the third watch of the night and then get into position for the attack. Take care that you do not hit any of our men."

Just before dawn Ba'ana launched his attack. Flaming arrows split the sky, landing on dozens of tents and setting them ablaze. As dazed enemies ran out of their tents, many were struck down. Before they could organize for a counterattack, Ba'ana's force disappeared into the night, erasing its tracks.

Melek, chief of the Midianite clan, was beside himself with anger and frustration. He shouted,

"Evil dogs! They won't even come out and fight like men. I have lost many of my men. Who are they?"

"We don't know."

"Well, find out now. They cannot get away with this kind of unfair trickery!"

"Yes, Melek, We will find out."

His aides returned puzzled.

"We found no tracks at all and no equipment of any kind. They must be a spirit force."

"Spirit, nothing!" Melek spat out angrily. "They were very human, but very devious. They must be found and killed, every one of them. Do you understand, you miserable sons of Moabite prostitutes?"

"Ah!" commented Ba'ana to his men. "You did well. We will now wait awhile and strike them right after they settle down for the night."

Two nights later they were again in position, silently awaiting the moment to attack. Since not many tents were left intact from the firestorm, Ba'ana's force aimed at hitting first the guards, and then the other Midianites asleep on their bed mats. Scouts had located the prisoners, guarded within a makeshift stockade outside of the main camp.

"We will first silently free them, after dispatching their guards, and then arm them," Ba'ana instructed his warriors. "They will be a welcome addition to our little force. Once they are with us, we will attack the camp as planned."

Dawn was just tinting the eastern sky a dark blue-grey as they reached the stockade and freed their colleagues. Ba'ana signaled them to total silence, as he and the others passed along weapons to them. Then they retreated to the hills to regroup and advise their newly freed comrades on the plan of attack. Joyous hugs were shared. Bows, arrows, slings and swords were checked. Then Ba'ana signaled for the attack to begin. Again, the Midianites were caught by surprise, with many of their number felled. Some of the Ba'ana's warriors ran to camels, loosing their ropes and shouting at them. Frightened, the camels bolted and ran off. And again, Ba'ana's troopers hid their tracks and melted into the hills.

Melek tore his robe in anger. He bellowed,

"I have lost my prisoners. And now I have lost my camels! And I still haven't seen a single one of those devils! Surely they are wretched Israelites. What are you standing around for? Go find them. Kill them all!"

"But, Sire!" one of his subordinates said, "Where do we look? We can't even find a footprint?"

"Footprint or no, find them!! You will go without food and water until you do, hear?"

"Yes, Sire," his warriors answered dejectedly.

They went out in teams in search of the enemy, but never came back. Each team was ambushed and shot down. Only two men survived to return to camp. Out of breath and consumed with fear, they told Melek,

"Sir, the enemy is out there in great numbers. Wherever we turned, they were waiting for us. We had no chance. You are right. They are accursed Israelites."

"Where did those demons gather up large numbers? The last we knew, they were only a few ragged nobodies. Even with our prisoners, they couldn't have numbered more than 30 or 40. Then, from where did this horde come?"

"We don't know, Sir."

"Of course you don't, you stupid sons of donkeys. If they numbered more than your fingers and toes, you couldn't even count them."

Melek cursed as he walked around their camp. Not much he could do at this point but gather up what few men he had left, along with as many arms as they could manage, and retreat back to safer Midianite ground.

Ba'ana led his victorious "horde" back to Tamar. They numbered fewer than 30. Arriving there exhausted, they surveyed the stark ruins of the fortress.

What should they do now? Ba'ana assembled his men and instructed them,

"We shall send a runner to Jerusalem, to report to King Solomon and his commanders. They will want to know the entire story and also, we will need to decide what to do about our fortress. We cannot rebuild all of it without help and materials, especially wood for the doors. You, Hanani, will be our envoy to the court. Rest tonight and tomorrow. Be prepared at dawn the next day to depart. I will send Joab with you. Meanwhile, I will write up a report and some recommendations. Now, dismissed! We will do what we can about food. All of you get some well-earned rest. Tomorrow we will do no work. On the following day we will begin to clear out the rubble from the gateway and the buildings. Dismissed."

After the extra day of rest Hanani was eager to be on his way. He stored the commander's scroll in a courier pouch, rolled up his bed mat, scrounged what little food he could manage to take, picked up his sword, bow and a quiver full of arrows, along with his lance, sling and several stones, and was ready to set out. Ba'ana wished him Elohim's special protection. Then he left the fortress at a trot, his friend Joab at his side.

Traveling rapidly, they journeyed long hours each day, resting at night in a well-hidden spot. It still took them into the fifth day to arrive at their destination, hot and exhausted. Hanani reported directly to the palace, handing over his message to one of the king's clerks. A guard then took both of them to a guest area in the palace, where they could bathe, put on palace garb and be prepared to eat at the king's table that night. Joel said,

"Bless Elohim. We'll be living in the lap of luxury at least for the night."

Eventually they were escorted to the king's private dining room and seated near the head of the table. When Solomon entered, all stood with head bowed until he was seated. With him were Azariah, Zadok, Abiathar and Zabud, priests and personal advisors; Elihoreph and Ahijah, secretaries; Jehoshaphat, recorder; Benaiah, commander-in-chief of the military forces; Ahishar, chief of the palace staff; and Adoniram, official in charge of forced labor. Although by now one of the ancient ones, the king still walked and sat with great dignity, showing little outward indications of his age.

"Quite an impressive assembly," noted Hanani, as he and Joab were introduced to the group. "I have never been around so many important people in my life. I hope my country ways don't betray me too much. But where are the women? We haven't seen any except servant girls."

Ahijah finally asked Hanani to share with the group present their situation at Tamar.

"Great king and noble leaders of our nation," he began humbly, "We are honored by the kindness you have shown us, by this feast and for the opportunity to share personally with you our understanding of our situation. First, we had to do battle against the Midianites, who attempted to storm the fortress. They were fought off by our small but courageous contingent of warriors. Then two of us, while on a hunting expedition, were accosted by Edomites, who took us captive to Sela. There we were imprisoned and held for ransom, as you may recall. We were freed when Commander Ba'ana called for warriors from all of the southern fortresses and Jerusalem. This combined force, using the tactics of Gideon of old, penetrated the stronghold at Sela and got us out safely.

"Upon our return to Tamar, we found, to our great dismay, that it had been overrun by a very large force of Midianites, who did much damage to the fortress and killed many of our colleagues, along with Ba'ana's aged mother, who had remained there to maintain his home. They captured fifteen of our men. Our commander, using bandit tactics, hit their camp on different nights with flaming arrows and other weapons and then ran their camels off. We were able to recapture our warriors and returned safely to Tamar, without a man lost."

"Our gratitude to your commander and to all of you," Solomon spoke up with a voice that still showed the power of a much younger man. "Your entire group will be rewarded. Now, what does Commander Ba'ana propose to do about the condition of the fortress?"

"Noble Sire, he wants to rebuild it, but will need both materials and skilled workmen. Most of the stones can be reused, but we will need all new timbers for the ceilings and especially, for the gates. They are only charred remains now."

"Tell your commander that he will have everything he needs. We will not only send skilled craftsmen, but also a servant girl, in some small way to replace his venerated mother in caring for his home. Do I understand that you no longer have a cook, nor many provisions?"

"That is true, Sire. We are almost without provisions and are only eating one meal a day, to conserve what we have."

Tamar

"We will immediately charge Azariah and Adoniram to provide personnel, building materials and provisions. Benaiah will reinforce your contingent with new warriors. Can you wait here until all is ready? Then you can guide our wagons to Tamar."

"Excellent, Most Noble King, and our deepest gratitude. Our entire force at Tamar will be overjoyed to receive such a bountiful response to our needs."

"Again," answered the king, "our deepest gratitude to your most courageous warriors. Please remain as our guests until all is ready for your departure."

"Thank you, Sire. Your generosity is overwhelming."

"It is nothing. Now, please leave us to our staff, while we begin to plan for the rebuilding of Tamar."

Hanani and Joab returned to their quarters gratified by the outcome of their audience with the king. They imagined it would take several days for the personnel and material to be rounded up. Meanwhile they would enjoy immensely those days. On one such day, while walking along the palace roof, they both finally spotted some of the harem women in their court.

"What beauties!" Hanani whistled. "I wonder what it would be like to be married to one of those. But what am I thinking? That would never happen, so I might as well quit dreaming. I do wish I had a mate, but there is no chance of that while I'm stationed at Tamar."

"Unless you want to count the nannies in our flock, there is not a female within days of our 'palace'," Joab replied with a grin.

scroll 10

An Affair of the Heart

Ba'ana and his warriors-turned-clean-up-crew finally did all they could to prepare for reconstruction. Building stones were stacked in rows. Salvaged timbers were leaning against a wall. Bits and pieces of debris had been carried out of the fortress and dumped in a pile some distance from its walls.

"Men," Ba'ana announced one evening, "we can now take a rest. We will resume our normal duties following the morrow."

"Thank you, Sir!" the troop shouted in unison. Then, dismissed, each man trudged to his bed mat and stretched out. Soon most were asleep, the courtyard reverberating with various levels of snoring.

The anticipated day of rest didn't materialize, however. The one guard placed in the re, built tower shouted,

"Wagons and troops coming, Sir! I think they are reinforcements and building materials."

"Warriors, put on your dress uniforms and present yourselves at attention for our guests."

Even before the wagons entered the fortress, the contingent was standing at parade rest in two rows. Hanani was the first to enter. He shouted his greetings to one and all, and then reported to Ba'ana:

"Sir, I have brought from the bounty of our great King Solomon building materials, a detachment of warriors, trained craftsmen, cooks, and a maiden to care for your house and provisions!"

"Excellent! Welcome to your desert inn! Warriors, you are indeed welcome. We will soon integrate you into our force here. Let us first, however, unload the provisions. I see you brought two cooks, so we will put them to work immediately. We need to feed this entire ravenous group. Craftsmen, oversee the unloading of materials. Warriors, assist the craftsmen with the unloading. Maiden, what is your name?"

"Hannah, Sir," she answered modestly.

"Hannah is a beautiful name, taken from the great Samuel's mother. You have a wonderful model to follow."

"I Know, Sir. And I try to live up to her example."

"And where is your home, Hannah?"

"Tirzah, in the north, Sir."

"Yes, I have been there. It is a lovely little town. Beware of one thing, Hannah. There are a lot of men here who haven't had the company of a woman in a long time. Be forewarned. I am instructing all of the men to treat you with respect and dignity."

"Thank you, Sir."

"Now, everyone to the work. You will be called when the meal is ready. Hannah, you may go to my residence, just outside of the entrance, and give it a general cleaning. My men have gotten rid of the debris and 'cleaned' it, but not to the level you probably require. If you need any supplies or help, please let me know. For now, you may take your meals with us."

"Thank you, Sir."

By time for the evening meal the wagons had been unloaded and the men had washed up. They sat down to a repast that had long been overdue. But before consuming it, Ba'ana led in a prayer:

> Let us bow before the Lord our maker. Let us praise Him for His bountiful provision. Let us thank Him for protecting us to this point. Let us ask for his blessing on our food and our lives. Amen.

The next morning Hanani organized the warriors into their watches. Ba'ana ordered those not on watch duty to assist the stonemasons and carpenters in their work. Soon everything was running smoothly; that is, relatively so. Some of the warriors didn't like the idea of being simple drudge servants. When they complained, Ba'ana responded sharply,

"Your task is to do what I order you to do! Right now I'm ordering you to work under the direction of the craftsmen. If anyone doesn't want to cooperate, I will find a job even more distasteful for you to do. Understood?"

"Yes, Sir," they growled and went back to their assignments.

An Affair of the Heart

Within a few weeks the new doors had been hung and the broken walls and roofs repaired. Ba'ana's house also received its needed repairs. He then moved back into it, having spent the interim in the barracks with his men. Much was to be done to make it livable again, but Hannah tackled it, singing songs from her hero, the legendary King David. All the men, and especially Hanani, appreciated hearing her singing. It gave a bit of color to their otherwise drab life at the fortress.

When he first met Hannah, Hanani was taken by her grace and beauty. His impression of her only increased with the passing of the days. He wondered, "Could she be the one for me?" It may not have been love at first sight, but before long serious interest in Hannah definitely pierced his heart.

However, he was hesitant to make any overt advances to her. It wasn't customary to initiate courtship toward a potential mate or to ignore one's parents in the choice of such a partner. A young man's family usually selected a suitable girl and arranged a marital agreement, with the required dowry being stipulated by her parents. Hanani was perplexed as to how to handle this problem-filled situation. He had no idea if she even noticed him. After all, she hadn't been there long and barely knew any of the fortress's personnel. To complicate matters, his parents were a long way off and, of course, had never met Hannah and her family.

And to further complicate this matter, most of the warriors had their eye on Hannah. That could be stiff competition, indeed. Hannah might well become the unknowing source of jealousy and hard feelings.

"I really think I want to pursue this matter, but what can I do? Hannah probably hasn't even noticed me, let alone taken any interest in me," Hanani mumbled. "How could I ever manage to present her to my mother and father, and to get the two sets of parents together? Perhaps I should seek Ba'ana's advice on this. He knows her better than the rest of us."

One day, alone with Ba'ana, he asked his opinion about this delicate matter.

"Sir, I, uh, I am interested in Hannah as a possible mate, but, as you can guess, the matter is difficult. Neither my parents nor hers are available. I have no dowry to speak of. And I could set off jealousy on the part of others here who may have an eye on her." With a sigh, he added, "Besides, I have no idea what her feelings are, if any, toward me. Sir, do you see any good solution to this matter?"

"Well, you do have some problems," Ba'ana chuckled. "I appreciate your interest in Hannah. If I were younger, I might try for her affections.

You are right about your companions. More than one has noticed Hannah. If you do win her affections, there may be some ill feelings, but that shouldn't deter you. As to the parents involved, there is no ready solution. She is from Tirzah and you are from Megiddo. Perhaps at some future date I can send you on a courier errand to Megiddo. There you can approach your parents about their meeting her parents and making the necessary arrangements."

"Wonderful, Sir!"

"But first you must unobtrusively get better acquainted with Hannah and build a relationship with her. I will assign you at times to guard my home or to escort her to the distant oasis to bring in our goats. That will give you opportunities alone with her. However, again I would advise you to be perfectly circumspect. What we don't want are rumors to begin circulating that could damage you both."

"Yes, Sir. I will be most careful. Thank you for your understanding help."

"Well, Hanani, I am a bit of a romantic at heart and won my wife by subtle means, which sometimes can work miracles. Believe me, I understand and wish you well in your quest."

Hanani spent many of his waking hours dreaming about how to get better acquainted with Hanna.

"Doesn't that name have a nice poetic ring to it, especially coupled with mine: Hanani and Hannah? Elohim must have made us for each other. Now, how do I go about convincing her of this?"

But suddenly he was jolted back to earth from his daydreams when he received new orders from Ba'ana.

scroll 11

Hanani's Heart on Hold

"Hanani," Ba'ana explained to his aide, "the fortress at Arad is being threatened by an unknown party of raiders. I'm sending you there with a few of our best warriors to aid the fortress in its impending battle."

"Yes, Sir!" Hanani answered, although not thrilled by the prospect. "Who will be in my force and when shall we leave?"

"I have already made a list of some capable, dependable men. Here. Look it over and see if you agree. You are to leave right after the morning meal tomorrow."

After glancing through the list, Hanani said, "These are all good men. I will be proud to lead them. Will you call them together and explain our mission?"

"Yes, I will, and I will also make it clear that you are in command. Your orders will be just as if I myself were there giving them."

"Thank you, Sir. We will be ready by daybreak."

The next day Hanani and nine other handpicked warriors, including Hanani's friends Joab and Isma'el, were well armed, well supplied and on their way to Arad, four days away. In order not to be observed, they traveled primarily during the night, hiding out during the day. A full moon facilitated their journey.

When they neared Arad, a wilderness fortress much like that at Tamar, but with a surrounding walled village, Hanani said,

"We will remain in ambush here, awaiting a possible encounter with these assailants. Jonas, slip on ahead in the dark and call out to the watchmen that you are from Tamar. Once admitted, explain our plan to the commander. Suggest to him that he engage the enemy, keeping its attention on the fortress, so that we can attack from the rear and then vanish quickly. Such a tactic has worked before, so we will try it again."

"Yes, Sir. I'm on my way."

There was nothing now to do except wait in hiding for the enemy to appear. They waited and waited, but no one showed up. Day after day passed without any signs of an invading force.

Then, when they were about to give up and go on into the fortress, their man on guard above them in the hills warbled a prearranged bird trill, repeating it three times. Hanani motioned to his men to be prepared for battle. Soon the mysterious invaders could be identified—Midianites!

"So! You are back for some more punishment, are you?" Hanani whispered. "Now, warriors, shoot your arrows with deadly precision. May our great El Shaddai protect us."

Within moments the rocks and trees in the area gave up a volley of arrows, and then a second volley. By the time the Midianites turned to face their new opponents, Hanani's force had disappeared. They then set up a new line of fire. As some of the Midianites came running toward them, they aimed from their cover and downed all of their pursuers. Hanani shouted and his warriors turned on a run toward the greatly reduced enemy force.

Just as they engaged the enemy, an arrow hit Hanani in the leg and he went down. Motioning his colleagues to continue the fight, he eased himself behind a boulder and prepared his weapons for defense.

"If this is my end, I will take as many of the enemy with me as possible," he breathed through teeth gritted against the pain.

His companions pressed the fight, forcing the enemy closer and closer to the fortress walls. Then they backed off and gave the defenders a clear field for their shots. More and more of the enemy fell. When their commander was hit, the few raiders left turned and fled, running into a barrage of arrows from Hanani. Not knowing how many warriors were behind that boulder, they hesitated, only to find the rest of Hanani's contingent surrounding them. They laid down their arms and surrendered.

Hanani was soon carried to the fortress, where he and the enemy commander were both treated for the wounds they had received in the battle. The commander was amazed that his enemies showed him such mercy. When he was well enough to travel, he was placed on a donkey and escorted, along with his captured troops, to Jerusalem. The captives were to be placed under military arrest and forced to do manual labor in one of the king's many building projects.

Hanani couldn't have asked for more diligent care than he received. He was soon ready to return to Tamar. The commander at Arad, Harim, thanked him and his warriors for their courageous service. He placed a message to Ba'ana in Hanani's hands, furnished his team with provisions for their return journey and sent them on their way, with Hanani given a donkey to ride.

Once back at Tamar, Hanani handed the message to Ba'ana. He read it over and then assembled his entire force.

"Warriors, I have here a message from Arad. It says this:

> Harim, commander of our great Solomon's fortress at Arad, to Ba'ana, commander at Tamar, greetings. I cannot speak too highly of the courage and dedication of the force you sent to our rescue. Your warriors ambushed the enemy—Midianites— killing a number of them and helping capture the remainder. Your leader, Hanani, showed excellent leadership, but was wounded. He remained with us until he was able to travel again. I wish him, his companions and all of you Elohim's richest blessings. Shalom.

"I add my congratulations to Hanani and all of his companions," Ba'ana announced. "They are hereby given a week of rest and an extra ration of food and wine. Now, you are dismissed!"

Hanani was still limping, but went in search of Hannah. Arriving at the commander's home, he called out to her, but got no answer.

"Sir, where is Hannah?" he hurriedly returned to the fortress and asked Ba'ana. "I have longed all of my journey to be back with her."

"I am so sorry, Hanani. She received a message from her family, telling her that her mother was desperately ill and that she was to come there as soon as possible. I sent her off with an escort several days ago. She should be back at Tirzah by now."

"Oh, no!" sighed Hanani, brokenhearted. "Will I ever see her again? I had no opportunity to express to her how I feel about her, and now it may be forever too late."

Tamar

Hannah sat beside her mother's bed, wiping her fevered brow. She was concerned about her mother, but also concerned about Hanani.

"I wish I could see him again." she sighed. "If I ever get back to Tamar, he may not even remember me. Or, even more likely, he may have been transferred elsewhere. I am sick at heart with love for him. What am I to do?"

"My daughter, what is troubling you? You seem lost in thought, or perhaps worry. Are you concerned about me?"

"Yes, dear mother, I am concerned about you, but also about my not being able to fulfill my duties at Tamar. My heart is divided between here and there."

"Hmmm," her mother pondered, "I sense a heart problem here. I wonder if there is something going on that she hasn't revealed to me."

One day, as Hanani had the day watch, mooning over his beloved, he saw a man approaching hurriedly on horseback. He arrived at the gate and identified himself as Jeroboam, formerly an official in the king's service. Hanani signaled to the gatekeeper to let him enter.

Once inside the fortress, Jeroboam asked for the commander. Ba'ana soon appeared.

scroll 12

A Fugitive Seeks Shelter

How may we help you?" Ba'ana asked. "Are you on official business for the king?"

"Well, to tell you the truth, I am fleeing from an enemy."

"And who is this enemy?"

"None other than King Solomon!"

"Do you mean to say that there is a price on your head by the head of our country?"

"That is right. I had been a man of standing in the court, serving as chief of the labor force for the entire house of Joseph. However, I could see that, as he has grown older, his rule has deteriorated. Moreover, a certain prophet named Ahijah approached me one day and informed me graphically that the kingdom would be torn apart during the reign of Solomon's son. I would be given ten of the tribes and he would have only Judah and little Benjamin as his territory. When the king heard about this, he tried to kill me, but I have escaped. I seek asylum, at least temporarily, in your fortress."

"We cannot permit this, Jeroboam. If the king were to find that we had sheltered a fugitive, we would be severely punished, perhaps even killed. You may pass the night. We will care for your mount and give you food and rest. But in the morning you must be on your way."

"Commander, I am disappointed in you, but will follow your orders. However, when I am ruler of Israel and you want anything of me, you will find I have a deaf ear to your request."

"So be it! Now, get your rest. You will need it for your journey ahead."

With that, Jeroboam was escorted to an alcove in the fortress, where a bed mat awaited him. He was told that food would be brought to him shortly.

Early the next morning he was on his way eastward, where he would link up with the Way of the Sea and head on it to Egypt. He was sure that Pharaoh Sheshonk, who was always eager to shelter any enemy of Israel, would take him in.

Day after day Hannah cared tenderly for her mother, but day after day she looked to the south, to see if, by some divine miracle, Hanani might appear.

"There is no reason why he should come, but I pray that he will. I miss him and I just might be in love with him. No, I *am* in love with him! But what good will that do? When my beloved mother is better, my family will want to select a man for me, but how can he ever be the man who has captured my heart?"

She sighed, as she again returned to her small home. She had to prepare another meal, fetch water and keep her mother bathed and medicated.

Day after day Hanani looked to the north and dreamed of being again with Hannah. He had begun to realize that she was definitely the woman for him, but he could see no way in which to talk with her and reveal what was really on his heart. He had little silver, no home and no chance to meet her parents and convince them that he was the man for her.

"Love of my life," he sighed, "How I long to see you again!"

"Hanani!" spoke up his colleague Parosh. "Wake up from your daydreams. It is time to change the guard."

"Sorry! My mind was far away."

"Yes, I could tell. You might as well have been in far-off Tarshish. Just what was occupying your mind?"

A Fugitive Seeks Shelter

"That is only for me to know," Hanani said, as he walked away, "but some day I may tell you."

Alone, he prayed,

"Great Elohim, I trust in you to provide a solution to my dilemma. If you will, bring Hannah back to me, or take me to her. I love her, but cannot express my love from this distant post. Is this too much to ask? You created the capacity to love in our hearts. Now, I pray, let not my love go unrequited. Amen and amen."

Then something happened to take his mind off of lovesickness. On an occasional day off from their dull routine at the fortress, small parties of warriors were permitted to go out in search of game. On one occasion Hanani was with four other warriors. They had no luck finding real game, but did shoot down some birds. With several hours on their hands before they had to return to the fortress, they decided to explore a cave in the nearby hills. Since it was dark in the cave, they made a fire by striking two stones together and creating a spark over a pile of dead brush. When a blaze was going well, they gathered up fallen tamarisk branches, smeared them with pitch from nearby trees and then set them afire.

With torches in hand, they entered the cave, leaving one of their partners at the entrance, to warn them of any approaching danger. Winding their way through the cave, they began to notice in its far recesses yellow-colored flecks and veins.

Upon examining them, Hanani shouted, "Gold! I think we have found gold."

scroll 13

Gold in Those Hills!

They all crowded around Hanani to take a look. Sure enough, it appeared to be gold and there was plenty of it. Now what should they do, dig out some of it and hide it away or report what they had found to the commander?

"I think the only honest thing to do," commented Hanani, "is to report this to Ba'ana. Perhaps he will permit our digging here and sharing some of it with all of our colleagues. I know he will want to send a good part of it to the king, but we should get some of it for discovering and mining it."

"I don't know," said Joab. "He may decide to leave it where it is, or to send all of it to the king. I guess, though, we will have to tell him about it."

They used their swords to carve out a segment of the rocky wall. Upon arriving back at the fortress, Hanani and his companions went to Ba'ana. Hanani explained,

"Sir, in our looking for game, we found a very small opening in the rock face of the mountain. We removed some stones, entered a sizeable cave and found this, which appears to be gold. There is a lot of it. We decided to close the hole for now. What should we do? Should we leave it alone, mine it, send it all to the king or send part of it to him and divide the rest among us?"

"Where is this cave? If it is in our jurisdiction, that is one thing. If it is in Edomite territory, we run a great risk, if we attempt to extract the gold."

"Sir, I believe it is in our territory, but close to the Edomite border."

"Hanani, this poses some real problems. Let me ponder on it and I will get back with you. Meanwhile, keep this to yourselves."

"Yes, Sir," Hanani answered for his team.

The next day Commander Ba'ana called his troop together and said,

"Some of our warriors have found gold in a cave. They closed it back up until we decided what to do with it. I have concluded that we should mine it, but only at night, with teams rotating. We will send it in small batches with couriers to the king. I will request that we be given permission to keep a part of it, or to receive a part of it back, as a recompense for our efforts. I do not know what he will decide. Meanwhile, we will draw lots for assignment to the cave."

All were talking at once, as they dreamed of great riches coming their way.

"Just a moment!" Ba'ana spoke up. "We are not rich yet and may never be. But let us proceed with the utmost caution on this. If word gets out, we will be drowned in people racing here in the hopes of becoming instantly wealthy. Now let us proceed with casting lots for the first crew."

That very night Hanani led the first team to the cave. It was soon opened and, with torches lit, the men entered the cave, all except a guard at the entrance. They carried digging tools left at the fortress from the reconstruction project and excitedly began to extract the gold-bearing rock. After several hours of labor, Hanani called a halt.

"You have done well, indeed, but we can only carry so much back and must be there before dawn catches up with us. Carry out your load in the bags you have brought. Then we will close the cave, erase our footprints near it and return to the fortress."

Ba'ana was very pleased with their work and gave them the day off to sleep. The next night another of the discovery team led more of the warriors to the cave, repeating the exercise.

When they had mined several bags full of the ore, Ba'ana commissioned Hanani, Joab and two others to take them to the king. The bags were loaded onto donkeys, along with provisions for the journey. Ba'ana instructed,

"Hanani, I want you to deliver this message to the king. It explains this whole matter and requests that a percentage of the refined gold be returned to us as a salary for our efforts. Once the gold has been delivered, three of you return here. Hanani, I have a message for the commander at Megiddo.

While you are there, you may spend several days with your family. And before you leave the region, you just might want to stop by Tirzah."

"Thank you, Sir, and especially for the opportunity to visit Tirzah," Hanani said with a broad smile.

"Just don't forget to return here. Now, all four of you be prepared to leave at dawn tomorrow."

"Yes, Sir!" they all echoed.

The next day this little troop was on its way, dressed, not in military gear, but in trader's clothing. This perhaps would make them a less likely target for enemy forces. To hide the gold ore, they filled the top of each bag with dates and other commodities.

Their route took them up the tortuous Scorpion Ascent and from there to the fortress at Araor, the villages of Carmel and Tekoa, and then on to Jerusalem, five full days away. They suffered no difficulties in the way of attacks on them, arriving in the capital during the day. They delivered their bags of gold to the king's palace manager, Abishar, and the message from Ba'ana to the king's secretary, Abijah.

While the others awaited a return message to Ba'ana, Hanani, impatient to be on his way, bid them shalom and turned northward, riding one of the donkeys they had used for carrying the ore. He went by way of Ramah, Shiloh, Shechem, Dothan and on from there to Megiddo, five more hard days' journey to the north.

After delivering the message to the fortress commander at Megiddo, Hanani explained that his family lived nearby. He would spend about three days there and return to pick up any response for Ba'ana. He then headed out, running, to his home. Imagine his parents' surprise when he walked in the door.

Shouting, "My son!" his mother ran to embrace him. "What are you doing here and in nonmilitary clothing? Is your service over already?"

scroll 14

A Commitment of Love

"No, my mother," Hanani answered, "I was sent secretly to Jerusalem and then on to Megiddo with a message, receiving permission to spend three days with you before returning."

"Wonderful! But you look too skinny. Aren't they feeding you properly?"

"Yes, mother. The fare is simple but sufficient. We work hard and sweat off any extra weight we might put on. For much of the year it is very hot there."

"Well, come and sit down. Your father and brothers will be in from the fields soon. We will have our evening meal very shortly. In honor of your visit, we will prepare a lamb, along with our own vegetables and one of my special sweets. How does that sound?"

"Great, mother. I have longed all of this time for one of your feasts."

When his father and brothers came in, all were excited about his presence and plied him with constant questions.

"Were you ever attacked? Did you kill any of our enemies? Were you wounded?"

"Wait, wait, wait! Let me take things in order from the time I left here. As you recall, I left Megiddo with nine other warriors in training. Then we marched to Jerusalem, where we joined other warriors and our new commander, Hoshea. I enjoyed my brief stay in Jerusalem. No, I didn't get to see King Solomon, nor any of his harem. I did visit our majestic temple, however.

Tamar

"Then we took a long march to Tamar, by way of the Negev, descending the steep Scorpion Ascent. We finally arrived there, to find it a small fortress in the midst of very hot and arid country. We met our fellow warriors already there and settled into a boring routine of watches.

"After some time had passed, Commander Hoshea took part of our company, along with his family, to Ezion-geber, a port on the Red Sea. I had the honor of being in command at Tamar until a new commander, Ba'ana, arrived. We did have an interesting battle with Midianites, driving them away from the fortress.

"One day Ba'ana sent two of us out to kill game for our group. We were accosted by a large force of Edomites, who took us captive to Sela, their stronghold. Ba'ana brought in reinforcements from other fortresses and attacked Sela, using the tactics of our ancestor Gideon. They worked as well for him as they had for Gideon. We were soon released and on our way back to Tamar.

"Arriving there, we found that our fortress had been overrun and largely destroyed. Many of our men had been killed, along with Ba'ana's aged mother. We went in hot pursuit of the enemy, to find out that they were Midianites, who had sought revenge against us for their earlier defeat. Ba'ana used bandit tactics to set their tents on fire, scatter their camels and free the prisoners they had taken. In a later skirmish with the Midianites I took an arrow in the leg. But with good care, I was soon healed."

"Let me see the scar; let me see it!" the boys all shouted. So he took off his leather leg guard and showed it to them. They were in awe of their "hero" brother, who had actually been wounded in battle.

How many Midianites did you kill?"

"Several, before my companions dispatched the rest.

"Now, back at Tamar, we discovered gold in a cave, mined some of it and a team of us brought it to the king. I was sent on to Megiddo, to deliver a message from Ba'ana. That explains why I am here. I cannot stay long. I have some business in Tirzah to attend to on the way back. Dear family, you will have to put up with me for three days."

His brothers were full of more questions. is His parents were overjoyed to have him back with the family. He was happy to be home again, but his time there dragged a bit for him. He was eager to get on to Tirzah, but for his family, his stay was all too short.

"My son, do you have to leave so soon?" his mother asked, as he prepared to leave again.

A Commitment of Love

"Yes, I have already stayed one more day than I intended. It is time to go."

"We will miss you so much!" his mother sighed.

His father, not one to show much outward emotion, gave him a quick embrace on his shoulders and wished him Elohim's blessings on his return journey. His brothers gave him proud hugs and urged him to kill more of Israel's enemies.

Hanani saluted his family, checked in at Megiddo and then set off, driving his donkey at a trot for Tirzah, two days away. Arriving there in the late afternoon of the second day, he began searching for Hannah.

Stopping by the village well, he asked everyone, "Do you know a Hannah? No, I don't have her father's name. What? There are three Hannahs in Tirzah?"

After several unsuccessful tries, he changed his approach.

"Well, the one I seek is young and beautiful. She went down south to Jerusalem and then on to Tamar to serve our commander, but returned here, due to her mother's ill health."

"Oh," said a maiden who had come to draw water, "you must be looking for Hannah daughter of Zechariah. If you like, I will take you there after I draw some water."

"Here, let me draw it for you."

"Thank you, kind Sir. Now, just follow me."

Before long he was standing at the door to Hannah's home, small, but normal for that and other like villages. In fact, it was very much like Hanani's own home near Megiddo, It had a single courtyard and entrance. It contained a central hallway, with walled-in areas along both sides. On one side were sleeping quarters and personal effects. On the other side was an area for keeping animals in during bad weather and at night. Across the back were a tiny kitchen area and storage space for grains and foodstuffs.

Hanani thanked the maiden and, his heart pounding in anticipation, called out,

"Shalom on this house."

A boy came to the door and asked him what his business was. He explained,

"I seek Hannah, daughter of Zechariah."

"How do you know her, Sir?"

"I am a warrior stationed at Tamar. She worked there for my commander for some time, until she was called back here because of her mother's illness."

"She isn't here right now, Sir, but should be back soon. Come in, rest and meet our mother."

With that Hanani thanked the youth and entered the house. The boy took him to his mother, who was sitting up on a sleeping mat, with cushions supporting her back. She smiled up at him and asked him to sit near her on a cushion. Then she asked,

"So, you wish to see my daughter. How well do you know her?"

"Not well, but I wish to know her much better. She is a wonderful, caring person."

"Yes, I agree, but there must be more to your story than that."

"Yes, I feel that I am in love with her, but have said nothing about this, except to my commander, who permitted me to stop off here in transit back from Megiddo. I understand the customs involved, so do not want to proceed without your knowledge and that of your husband. My parents live near Megiddo, so I expect they will need to come here to make the marriage arrangements.

"However, I don't know her feelings toward me, so until that is determined, I would not want to pursue this further. My parents were in love well before they married. Fortunately, their two sets of parents were understanding and gave their consent to the marriage. So I have a family precedent for marrying for love instead of by family arrangement."

"I appreciate that, my son. When Hannah comes in, we will have a talk. You must know that my husband died several years ago, so my permission is all that is required."

"My condolences, mother of Hannah."

"Thank you. Now, for some questions. First, are you a faithful son of the Covenant?"

"As faithful as I can be stationed at a very remote fortress."

"If you were married to my Hannah, how would you treat her?"

"With the utmost tenderness."

"Your possessions . . . Do you have any land, jewelry, gold or silver?"

"I have saved up the silver from my salary. It isn't much, but I continue adding to it. As for land, I am the firstborn of my farming parents, so will inherit their lands near Megiddo. I have no jewelry, but possibly will have some gold coming my way. I will know soon about that."

A Commitment of Love

"I have heard how warriors act. Do you ever get drunk? Do you fraternize with loose women?"

"No, mother of Hannah, on both questions. I drink very little and have never been intimate with any woman."

"How do your commander and fellow warriors look on you?"

"I feel uncomfortable putting words in their mouths, but for some time I was interim commander and now serve as the assistant to our new commander. He has entrusted me with a number of responsibilities. My companions also trust me."

"Very good. One more question. You appear to be somewhat educated. Are you literate?"

"Yes, mother."

Then they heard someone coming. They both turned and looked up to see Hannah framed in the doorway.

"Hanani!" she exclaimed. "How . . . how did you get here?"

"Lovely Hannah," he answered, smiling broadly, "I was sent as a courier to Megiddo. Commander Ba'ana gave me permission to spend some time with my family and then to stop here."

"You are not in uniform. Are you still serving at Tamar?"

"Yes, dear Hannah, I came with three companions on an important mission to the king's palace. We traveled in the disguise of merchants, so as not to draw so much attention to ourselves."

Just then Hannah's mother interrupted. She turned to Hannah and asked her without preamble,

"My daughter, do you love this man? Is he the one you have watched for almost daily since you came back home? I may be ill, but am still observant."

Hannah blushed and stammered,

"My mother, I . . . I . . . have loved him for a long time, but he didn't know it. Now what do I do?"

"Since I already know where his heart lies, I would suggest that you confess your love to each other and seal your relationship with a kiss. Go on, don't be shy!"

The two fell into each other's arms and whispered their vows of eternal love and devotion.

"Good," Isabel said. "Now we can get down to the details."

Hanani promised to have his parents come to Tirzah to work out the mohar and wedding arrangements. He talked about the mandatory nuptial year of waiting. That would take him to the end of his second year of military service.

"For my third and final year of service, I will take Hannah back with me to Tamar. I imagine that our commander will gladly let us live in his home, since he is alone, and Hannah can keep house and cook for us. That is, if she is willing. After my service is completed there, we will talk about where to settle."

"I will go anywhere with you, my love," Hannah shyly answered.

Her mother spoke up,

"We must have a special dinner in honor of our guest and perhaps soon to be a member of our family. Hannah, will you prepare it?"

"Gladly, dear mother."

She then squeezed Hanani's hand and went to the cooking area to begin preparing the dinner. Not knowing just what to do at this point, Hanani sat back down.

Hannah's younger brother, Enosh, came in then and began firing away at Hanani with questions of his own.

"Sir, have you ever been in a battle?"

"More than one, I'm afraid."

"Have you ever killed anybody?"

"That's the nature of war. I have killed, I have been captured and I have been wounded."

"Wounded? May I see your scar?

"Son," Isabel scolded, "you are being much too inquisitive!"

"It's alright. See, here is the arrow wound. It wasn't such a big thing, really."

"How were you captured?"

"Well, it sounds pretty silly, but two of us were out hunting game, when we were ambushed and taken captive to Sela, the Edomite stronghold. Our commander, Ba'ana, recruited volunteers from other fortresses and used our illustrious ancestor Gideon's tactics to frighten the enemy in the dead of night. It worked quite well."

"Your commander is a very smart man."

"Yes, and he is also courageous. It is a real pleasure to serve under him."

"I want to be a warrior like you, Hanani."

"Well, Enosh, it isn't all battles and courageous deeds. It is also tedious watches on fortress walls, often in the middle of the night. It is terrible heat, strong winds and sand storms. Food is very plain. Wine runs out and we are reduced to just water, sometimes bad water. There is no place to go and almost nothing to do at night. We play mancala, cast lots, wrestle and throw a ball around the courtyard. We also compete at shooting arrows, using the sling and throwing lances. So you see, it is not all dreary work, far from it, but it has its boring and dangerous sides. Altogether, it is good discipline and difficult service."

"I still want to serve!"

"Very well. I will submit your name to my commander for future recruitment."

"Will you, really? Thank you so much."

"Remember how you thanked me when you are on duty at some Elohim-forsaken outpost."

Just then three more brothers, all younger, came in from tending the family's sheep. They all clamored to find out everything about Hanani, so he found himself repeating much of what he had already told.

"The meal is ready," Hannah finally called out.

The boys made a hasty run to the low table spread in the central corridor, plopping down on cushions. They all wanted Hanani to sit by them, but Isabel motioned him to take the cushion at the table's head, the place of honor. She then asked him to lead a prayer of thanksgiving, which he did earnestly and with emotion.

Hannah had asked Enosh to kill one of the lambs, which she roasted to perfection. This, with vegetables from their garden and moist round bread smothered in honey, made for a very satisfying meal, washed down with aged wine.

"My Hannah," announced Hanani after a loud belch of satisfaction, "I knew you could cook, but this was extraordinary. I think I am getting far more in a future mate than I had imagined."

"Hush, Hanani. You are making me blush!"

"Well, it's true."

Hanani remained there as long as he dared, but finally said that he had to get back to his post. All begged him to stay longer, and none more so than Hannah. He handed her a message to be delivered to his parents, announcing his wedding plans and asking them to come to Tirzah as soon as possible.

"Could Enosh possibly find a companion and carry this message to my home?"

"Oh, yes," Enosh answered. "It will be a pleasure to do this."

"Thank you, Enosh."

Hannah accompanied Hanani out of the village, to the raised eyebrows of several matrons.

"It's alright," Hannah laughed. "We're to be wed."

When they were out of sight of the village, Hannah delayed his departure with a lingering kiss and an ardent prayer for his safety. He finally hugged her one more time, turned and rode steadily away. When would they see each other again?

Hannah was hardly back in her home when the village gossips descended on her mother.

"Who is this man your daughter is seeing?" they asked Isabel. "Who is his father? . . . Where does he live? . . . How did they come to know each other? . . . Are they having intimate relations?" . . . What have you done to stop this?"

"Wait just a moment!" she answered. "They are formally committed to marriage, with my blessings. His name is Hanani. He is from Megiddo and is a warrior in the king's service, stationed in the far south. They met when Hannah was there caring for the commander's home. All is legitimate, so I hope you spread this message around our town, in place of any bad-mouthing that you might be tempted to do."

"Well!" one old crone croaked. "You don't need to get uppity with us! We are only trying to protect your name and our town's reputation."

"Oh, I'm sure you are, but in this case, you may rest easy, knowing that my reputation remains pure, as do his and that of my daughter. One year from now you may help me prepare for the nuptial celebration and feast."

That captured their interest and they all began to offer suggestions for the big event. Finally, they hobbled out in high spirits. It wasn't every day that a marriage took place in their village, so they were eager to be a part of it.

Meanwhile, arriving back in Jerusalem, Hanani was told that his companions had returned to Tamar. He didn't tarry there long, picking up a message from the king to his commander, and was soon heading back to the fortress and his company.

scroll 15

The Lions Are out Tonight

"Shalom!" Hanani shouted, as he approached Tamar.

"Welcome back, Hanani," answered a guard on the tower. Shouting down into the fortress, he said, "Open the gates for him."

Hanani was soon in the midst of his companions, who were crowding around him.

"What news do you bring us?" asked one.

"I guess the biggest news is that I am to marry."

"Congratulations. Do we know her?"

"You should. She is Hannah, who was here for a time."

"Hannah? That beautiful maiden? How did you get so fortunate?"

"It must have been Elohim's doing, because I can claim little credit for it. I stopped by Hannah's home in Tirzah, on the way back from Megiddo. It soon turned out that she loves me and I realized how much I love her. Her widowed mother gave her consent for our marriage, so arrangements are being made for our official vows a year from now."

"You are one lucky warrior, Hanani!"

"What is this all about?" asked Ba'ana, as he walked up.

"Sir, Hanani has just announced his impending marriage to Hannah."

"That is no surprise. I already knew what was on his mind and gave him permission to visit her home in Tirzah. My best wishes, Hanani."

"Thank you, Sir. Here is a message from the commander at Megiddo and one from our great ruler."

"I will read them soon. Meanwhile, the gold we mined turned out to be good quality. The king has agreed to return a fifth of the smelted gold to us and gave us permission to continue mining. He will send a team of men here to do the bulk of the work and transport the ore back to the capital. That will relieve us of much of our own effort in getting out the gold. Of course, we will still serve as a guard for the miners and assist them as needed."

"Excellent, Sir!"

The next morning Ba'ana called out his warriors and announced,

"The ten of you who have been here the longest are to go to Megiddo, where you will train a new class of warriors in preparation. Ten from there will be transferred to Tamar. Hanani, you are to meet them at the fortress in Jerusalem and escort them here."

"Yes, Sir! When am I to leave?"

"I will give you a day in which to rest up from your recent travel. Early on the third day you are to go. Take a donkey and dress as a merchant, but carry your uniform with you. Once at the capital, put it on. I'm sending a message with you to the commander there about this matter. You and the new contingent are to bring back supplies for us, and also guide the miners here. There should be about six on their team. They, too, will be bringing supplies, along with their tools. Understood?"

"Yes, Sir, and thank you."

Hanani then washed up and prepared for the evening meal. Following it, he sought out his bed mat and gratefully stretched out on it.

The second morning later he shouted "Shalom" to his companions, saluted Ba'ana, who wished him Elohim's richest blessings, and headed out toward Scorpion Ascent, leading his donkey. During the ascent he had an encounter with a poisonous serpent, which he dispatched quickly. He had little trouble beyond that, except for the accursed donkey, which had a mind of its own.

"You contrary beast!" he shouted." If you continue to give me trouble, I will give you a beating. Do you understand?"

All he got in answer was a loud bray. He cut a slender limb from a tree and brandished it in the donkey's face. That seemed to help a bit, because at least for the rest of that day climbing the ascent, the beast was fairly cooperative. Later, however, he had to give it a whipping, just to establish who was in charge.

The Lions Are out Tonight

He arrived in Jerusalem without further incident and reported to the commander of the fortress there. He was shown to a cubicle in which he could sleep. Water was provided him for an ablution.

Two days later the new additions to the Tamar forces arrived. Meanwhile, Adoniram, the king's chief of labor, called out the six miners who had been promised to Ba'ana. Hanani met them and gave them a brief description of Tamar and the mine. They were a sturdy and tough-looking crew. One would not want to tangle with them, Hanani surmised.

"We must be ready to travel by early on the morrow," Hanani announced to the military recruits and the miners. "Each of us will manage a donkey and the supplies it carries. We must be well-armed, even you miners, for as we go farther south, we will be subject to raids by Edomites, Amalekites and Midianites, and perhaps a few other assorted troublemakers. Miners, can you handle a bow, sling or sword?"

"Yes," one responded. "We can knock out a lion's eye with the sling."

"Very good. Be sure you have a supply of stones with you and be alert at all times. If you do not have a sword, or at least a knife, obtain one from the commander here. We will stop each night in a secluded spot and have guards posted. Now, make your final preparations for departure."

The next day the warriors, dressed in their battle gear, divided up, some leading the group behind Hanani and the remainder acting as a rear guard or leading their donkeys beside the miners, giving them protection.

All went well until the third evening. Just after the group stopped for the night, a pride of lionesses streaked out of the dusk to down a donkey.

"Quickly!" shouted Hanani. "Kill them!"

In only a moment's time arrows were flying and stones were being slung, with devastating effect. Four of the five animals were downed, with the fifth running away as fast as she could. The donkey that had been attacked was mauled some, but otherwise survived. His wounds were cleaned and treated with salves.

"Thank you, men," Hanani said to the group. "You acted quickly and accurately. If these had been enemy fighters, they would have suffered the same fate."

Near evening on the sixth day they arrived at Tamar, to be greeted happily by the personnel there.

"Welcome, Hanani," Ba'ana said. "Did you have any difficulties?"

"None, Sir, except for a lioness attack. Four of the five creatures will never attack again. Our only casualty was a donkey, but he is mending satisfactorily, except for being easily spooked now."

"I see you have brought the replacements and the miners. Welcome to all of you. Unpack your animals and personal goods. Wash up. We will eat shortly. Afterward, we will find sleeping places for you."

The next day the ten warriors with the most tenure were sent off to Megiddo with the prayers and best wishes of their comrades. The miners were led to the gold dig by some of the warriors, who also helped them with their tools. Ba'ana placed the new warriors in Hanani's hands to orient.

"We will begin by putting you through a typical routine," Hanani told them. "You will each rotate with the others on guard duty, day and night. I will post a new schedule for this. Incidentally, if you haven't already sensed the fact, this is not really a 'fun' fortress. The weather is cruel, vicious sandstorms come our way and life is tedious most of the time.

"However, there are moments of excitement. You may be called upon to engage in battle or help with other matters outside of the routine. You are to keep your weapons in good condition and near you at all times. We never know what tomorrow, or even today, may bring. Now, what is your special ability when it comes to weapons?"

"We are adept at swordsmanship, throwing a lance and using a sling," one of replacement warriors answered. This was welcome news, because it meant that they would be versatile in a battle situation. They were as yet unproven in warfare, but he hoped that they would stand up well when a battle came. Meanwhile, he would test them, to see just how adept they really were.

For a long time things were again calm, too calm . . .

scroll 16

The King Is Dead! Long Live the King!

"Ho, the fortress!" shouted a courier, as he approached on horseback. His mount was covered with sweat, as was the courier, from the strenuous and rapid trip.

"Welcome, courier!" Ba'ana said. "What tidings do you bring us?"

"Not good tidings, Sir. Our great King Solomon has died and the country is in chaos. Commander-in-chief Benaiah has ordered 40 days of official mourning. He has also ordered that a contingent of ten warriors from each fortress be sent immediately to the capital, to participate in the official burial proceedings and to keep the peace until the new king is crowned."

"Very well, but they will not be sent today. It is too late in the afternoon to begin such a journey. As for you, stay here long enough to rest up. We will provide for you and your mount."

"Thank you, Sir. That is very kind of you."

"It is nothing. Now, bathe and get your rest. Food will be brought to you. Hanani, as second in command, it will be your task to select the warriors to go. Then you will lead them."

"Yes, Sir. We will leave at daybreak."

Right after dawn, Hanani and nine other warriors were fully dressed, armed and equipped for the journey. Ba'ana spoke to them,

"You have all been selected for this assignment because you are capable and courageous, as well as disciplined. Hanani is your commander. Obey him as you would obey me. Now, go and may our blessed Elohim guide and protect you."

Tamar

With plenty of donkeys on hand, each man had one to ride. This was a mixed blessing, because some of the donkeys objected to their human cargo. Also, most of the men had ridden very little. After the first day on the trail, they were sore. The next day they decided to walk and give themselves a chance to heal.

Still, they arrived in Jerusalem in good time and reported to the commander-in-chief. He welcomed them and showed them to quarters in the barracks. Beginning the next day, they were to be part of a force that would surround the capital, protecting its walls and screening all who were entering the city. They would also serve as an honor guard during the official funerary services and delivery of the body to its burial place.

The commander-in-chief explained to them,

"During a change of kingship, it is entirely possible that some rebellious elements will attempt to take control of the kingdom by force. You must be ready for any such eventuality. We will begin immediately a constant watch over the city, palace and temple. Your assignments by fortresses represented will be posted today. You will then immediately begin your watch. Dismissed!"

Hanani's contingent was assigned to the Old Gate, nearest to the temple itself. He told his warriors,

"We will begin rotating watches at the Old Gate. It is especially vulnerable, since it is near both the temple and the king's palace complex. It is an honor to be given this task. Let us therefore be especially diligent in fulfilling it."

"Yes, Sir!" answered his troop.

"So the great Solomon is dead!" Jeroboam said to his friends, as they sat in self-imposed exile in Egypt. "It is time for us to return and put some pressure on his successor, his son Rehoboam, for change."

They were soon on their way back to Jerusalem. During their journey they discussed how best to bring about change.

"Isn't the greatest complaint we had against Solomon," asked Jeroboam, "is his very high taxation? I believe we should solicit support from all the elders of Israel and demand that taxes be lowered."

The King Is Dead! Long Live the King!

They agreed with him and planned ways in which to recruit leaders in Israel to side with them. Now arriving before the city's massive wall, they were questioned by guards at the Fountain Gate their purpose. Jeroboam answered,

"We are former officials in the government and are here to pay homage to the memory of King Solomon."

"Enter, then," one of the guards answered.

Jeroboam's party was soon busy contacting all of the elders of Israel that they could locate. Their appeal for a lowered tax rate resonated with these greybeards and they agreed to go as a group to seek an audience with Rehoboam. Then they advised Jeroboam's group,

"But only after our noble King Solomon is buried and the period of official mourning has ended."

"Very well," Jeroboam said. "We will abide by your request."

"Attention!" shouted Hanani, as he prepared his contingent to march in the funeral procession for King Solomon. His warriors were dressed smartly in new garb furnished by the palace. Their weapons were polished and Hanani held aloft a banner identifying them as the Tamar unit.

At a signal from Commander-in-chief Benaiah, Hanani's troop took its place in its assigned spot and marched, in a slow cadence marked by the muffled beat of a drum. The procession itself began at the palace. An honor guard composed of palace military officials led the way, followed by the royal family—a multitude of persons—the king's government officials and the funeral bier itself. The body of the great king Solomon was dressed in a royal robe. Around his neck was a golden chain and pendant that represented his temporal authority. On his head was a magnificent crown.

Then came the guard from Jerusalem itself. Some distance back, Hanani's Tamar unit marched proudly but reverently. Other units preceded and followed his. Finally, the rear guard was made up of personnel from Megiddo. The funerary march moved slowly through the Horse Gate and down into the Kidron Valley toward the sepulcher where they would bury their leader. The wail of mourners filled the area, echoing off the city walls and the slopes of the valley.

Tamar

Arriving at the king's ornate tomb, his honor guard lifted the bier gently and carried it into the rock-hewn sepulcher carved out for his remains. His body was placed on a shelf and his royal garb was removed, replaced by linen strips, saturated with exotic spices such as myrrh and aloes. His head was wrapped in a sheath that covered it completely. His outer royal garments were then replaced on his corpse. When their task was completed, those who performed this last service backed out of the tomb, bowing in honor of his memory. With the help of some troopers, they rolled a huge round stone in front of the tomb's opening and sealed it with pitch.

Azariah the priest then pronounced a prayer and chanted one of Solomon's own psalms:

> Long may he live!
> May gold from Sheba be given him.
> May people ever pray for him
> And bless him all day long . . .
> May his name endure forever;
> May it continue as long as the sun.
> All nations will be blessed through him,
> And they will call him blessed.

The entire procession finally returned to the city and dispersed. Hanani and his unit were instructed to remain through the crowning of Solomon's successor and his firm establishment on the throne. They then made their way to the fortress and shed their processional dress.

"How long will we be here?" asked one of his warriors.

"I don't know," Hanani said, "but I would guess we will be here for several Sabbaths."

They all settled in for a quiet period of duty. This gave them time to explore the capital and its environs. They visited as a group the glorious golden temple. There they pooled a few pieces of silver and bought a lamb to present to the priests as a sacrifice in memory of the king.

The forty days of official mourning were over. Rehoboam had gone to Shechem, where he was crowned king in place of his father. He then returned to the city, resplendent in his rich robes and golden crown, riding on a white mount. He dismounted before the palace, entered it with his train of officials and sat down on his father's gold-and-ivory throne.

The elders decided that now was a good time to approach him, while he was still very new on the throne and had not yet established his rule. They asked Jeroboam and his party to accompany them to seek an audience with the young king. The newly installed chief of palace protocol, Shecaniah, escorted them to the throne room, where the 41-year-old Rehoboam sat in haughty splendor.

"And what is your petition, elders of Israel? Jeroboam, what are you doing here? As I recall, you fled the wrath of my father."

"O King Rehoboam, may you live forever. May your glory exceed even that of your father."

"Quit your platitudes and get on with it."

"Sire, your father put a heavy yoke of taxation and harsh labor on us. Now we appeal to you to lighten this load and we will be your faithful servants."

"So that is it? You want to get out from under the king's taxation? Return in three days and I will give you my answer."

Rehoboam then went to the aged ministers of Solomon, asking them how he should answer this request. They responded,

"If you will be a servant to these people and give them a favorable answer, they will always be your faithful followers."

Rehoboam wasn't really hearing them. Instead, he turned to his cronies and asked them how he should answer the elders.

"Tell them," they replied, 'my little finger is thicker than my father's waist. My father laid on you a heavy yoke; I will make it even heavier. My father scourged you with whips; I will scourge you with scorpions.'"

Rehoboam passed on these harsh words to Jeroboam and the elders. When they and all Israel realized that the king refused to listen to them, they angrily told him,

"What share do we have in David, what part do we have in Jesse's son? To your tents, O Israel! Look after your own house, David's offspring!"

The northern tribal leaders left in white-hot anger. After hasty consultations, they chose Jeroboam to become their king. He was soon crowned and took his place on a new throne at Shechem. Only the tribes of Judah and Benjamin, along with a number of the Levites and priests, remained loyal to the House of David. Rehoboam, in a rage, mustered all of the military personnel of Judah and Benjamin to war against the rebels.

Hanani was aghast at this order. He would be forced to fight against his own people of the north! How could he justify this? Yet, he had sworn loyalty to the House of David when he entered military service. He soon found himself and his troops in battle formation.

However, he was saved from the dilemma of fighting against his own. Rehoboam received a prophetic message from Shemaiah, the man of God. The prophet told him,

"Do not go into battle against your brothers, for this is Elohim's doing. Go home!"

Fortunately, the king listened to him and so sent his warriors back to their fortresses. The problem was that they no longer controlled Megiddo and other fortresses in the north. Some of them had no place to go, unless they returned home, abandoning Rehoboam and his kingdom.

"What shall I do?" asked Hanani to himself. I owe a responsibility to Ba'ana and our force at Tamar. But how can I ever go home? How can I see Hannah again and marry her?"

He was greatly troubled as he took his contingent back to Tamar. When they arrived, he reported in to Ba'ana. He then brought up this difficult dilemma to the commander.

"What should I do? My family and my beloved Hannah are now in a foreign country. Can I even enter it safely?"

"I don't know, Hanani. I understand your difficulty, but have no answer for it. Remain here in service and I will see if there is a way to solve this matter."

"Thank you, Sir."

A few days later Ba'ana called Hanani to his cubicle. He suggested,

"Hanani, I think I have a solution to your problem of divided loyalties. Why don't we try to smuggle your family and Hannah's to Judah?"

scroll 17

Hanani Turns Smuggler

BA'ANA EXPLAINED HIS SUGGESTION,
"I understand that Jeroboam has already set up official calf idols and shrines, so Elohim-fearing people will want to flee from there as quickly as possible. I believe that they can still move freely down through Israel. When they approach the border, they will have to cross at night, because I suspect there are border guards already commissioned to stop any such movements into Judah."

"Wonderful idea, Sir, but how will they know to do this?"

"Simple, my boy. You will go there and will guide them. Entering Israel should be no problem. Just go in nonmilitary garb and explain, if you are stopped, that you are from the tribe of Zebulon and are returning to your home in Megiddo."

"Thank you so much, Sir. I will prepare to leave immediately."

True to his word, early the next day Hanani had packed his necessary gear and had loaded two donkeys with gold ore, to deliver to the capital. He was to be accompanied by guards, to protect both him and his cargo. Ba'ana gave him a bag of the gold that had been returned to the fortress. He could use it to cover any expenses involved in the move. After reporting in to Jerusalem, Hanani would then take the donkeys alone on to Megiddo and Tirzah, to help transport the two families south.

Hanani had no trouble getting to Jerusalem. When he delivered the gold ore, the newly appointed court treasurer rejected it, having received no orders in regard to it.

"What is this all about?" he asked. "We have plenty of rock here already. We have no need of more. Besides, I have only your word that it is gold ore. Those flecks in it could be sulfur or pyrite, for all I know. Now, get along and waste no more of my time."

"Alright, then," Hanani said, "If that is the way it is, I will take it with me."

He headed on north as quickly as possible, before the treasurer could change his mind. He had no difficulty crossing the new border and finally arrived at Megiddo. There he hunted up a goldsmith, who agreed to burn out the gold for a percentage. He told Hanani that he would have the refined gold ready in two days.

Hanani thanked him and turned to leave. However, the goldsmith, who was examining the ore, asked him,

"But where did you find this quality gold ore?"

"In the Negev of far south Judah," he answered. Then he left and guided his donkeys along the familiar path toward home. Arriving there, he hailed the house.

"Hanani, my son!" his mother greeted him. "So good to see you, but what are you doing here, and with these donkeys?" The girls joined her, curious about his visit.

"This evening, when we are all together, I will explain everything. Right now I need to rest a bit."

"Of course, son. I will get out a bed mat for you. Would you like anything else?"

"Just a little wine, to help me unwind."

"I will bring you some."

"Thank you, mother. It is good to be home."

After Hanani had napped and cleaned up, he felt more refreshed. Shortly later, his father and brothers came in, surprised to see him.

"What are you doing here?" they asked almost in unison.

"Well, since we are all here, I can tell you that I'm on a special mission to take all of you to Judah. Now that the kingdom has divided and Jeroboam has introduced idolatry, it is no longer advisable for Elohim-fearing people to remain here."

"But our home is here and our little plot of land is here," his father objected.

Hanani Turns Smuggler

"I know and perhaps you can return to it one day, but I think it wise right now for you to move to Judah. At least there you will have the temple and faithful priests available, as well as the traditional feast days."

"What are you saying about King Jeroboam's introducing idolatry? We have heard nothing about that."

"Yes, he has set up golden calves and shrines at Bethel and Dan. He has placed his own illegitimate priests in service. My commander heard that he did this to keep the people of Israel from going to the temple to worship, and perhaps being enticed back under King Rehoboam's control. He has made it convenient for them to do their worshiping and sacrificing by erecting shrines near the northern border and near the southern border."

"In the name of Adonai," his father exploded, "may Jeroboam be cursed for this blatant act of idolatry!"

"That is exactly why faithful worshipers of Adonai will no longer be welcome here."

"We will discuss it further, son. Now let us prepare for our evening meal."

As they gathered around the low table, the father led the family in a Shema.

Then his mother, who was always a great cook, outdid herself in his honor. She served lamb, flat cakes, roasted wheat grains, lentils, lettuce, olives, onions and honey. She brought out her best wine. It was truly a satisfying meal, which elicited a complimentary remark from Hanani.

"Dear mother, this is one of the best meals I have ever eaten. It is truly a banquet, especially compared to our very plain fare at Tamar."

"Thank you, my son. I am happy you liked it."

"Now, mother and father," he said, "since we are all mellow after our feast, has a message come to you from Tirzah?"

"Yes, my son," his father answered, "but we haven't responded to it yet. What is this about your wanting to marry a girl from there, one we don't even know? How did you meet her?"

"She was a serving girl in our commander's home. I was taken, not only by her exceptional beauty and grace, but by her mind and heart. Over a period of time I realized that I loved her, but by then she had returned home to care for her invalid mother. On my last trip here I stopped off in Tirzah and discovered that she loved me, too. Her widowed and saintly mother gave her blessing to our marriage. Now all we need to do is to get you together with her to agree upon the mohar. My intention was to leave her with her family for the obligatory year of betrothal, then marry her and take her to Tamar for my final year of service there. Now that things have changed, my intention is to convince her and her family to accompany us to Judah."

"So you want to uproot two families, not just one! And how will we sustain ourselves on your humble warrior's salary?"

"You won't have to, my father. We discovered and are mining a rich deposit of gold near Tamar. My share of it has come to an impressive amount. In fact, I will receive even more shortly."

"That will have a considerable bearing on our decision, my son."

Two days later Hanani went back to the goldsmith and, giving him a tenth of the yield, left with the sizeable remainder in donkey saddlebags, well hidden under items of clothing and food.

Finally, he asked his father if he had decided about the move.

"Son, I have arranged with my nephew Joash to live here and care for our place. We will go with you, but give us two more days to make preparations."

"I am grateful for your decision and will gladly wait two more days."

"But why are you moving to far-off Judah?" the neighbors all asked, "This is your tribal land and we are your friends."

Amran explained to them about Jeroboam's idolatry, suggesting,

"You, too, may want to leave this land. If so, we will be glad to welcome you to our new home. After we are settled there, we will send a message to you about our location and life there."

The family was finally ready to make its move, with the two donkeys, joined by two others Hanani bought, well laden with household goods, clothing, bed mats, food and other items. Neighbors gathered around them to express regret at their move, but also to wish them a safe sojourn. Now, finally, they were on their way to Tirzah, the boys leading their small flock of sheep and whooping with delight over the adventure before them.

After two days' journey, they arrived at Hannah's home. Again, she was overwhelmed to see her man and also, finally to meet his family.

"Hanani, this is a surprise! How did you manage to visit us? Is this your family? And why are all of these goods piled high on donkeys?"

"Dear Hannah, yes, this is my family—my father, Amran, my mother, Rachel, my younger brothers, Gunih, Hezron and Serah; and my sisters, Carmih and Dinah."

Hanani Turns Smuggler

"Shalom. I am so happy to meet you, father, mother, brothers and sisters of Hanani. I have heard many good things about you."

"Shalom, Hannah," Amran said. "We too are happy to meet you, especially because of what we hear about Hanani's intentions toward you."

"But Hanani," Hannah said, "you haven't explained to me what is going on."

"First, my Hannah, I want my family to get to know your mother and family."

"Yes, of course.. My mother is still not fully recovered from an illness, so remains indoors." Showing her visitors into the house, she said, "Mother, we have guests, Hanani and his family."

"Welcome to our humble home, family of Hanani."

Hanani then introduced his family to Isabel. When they were all comfortably seated on cushions, all except two of Hanani's brothers, who were tending their flock, Hannah again asked what was going on. Hanani explained,

"Israel and Judah have separated. Rehoboam son of Solomon is on the throne in Jerusalem. Jeroboam, one of Solomon's officials, led Israel away from Judah, forming a new nation, with him serving as its king. Not long afterward he instituted calf-worship as the state religion, setting up shrines in Bethel and Dan. True worshipers of Elohim are no longer safe here. Moreover, our mighty Elohim will not permit this for long, but will bring disaster on Israel. For these reasons, I am taking my family to Judah, which still has the temple and the official priesthood ordained through our great leader Moses. We come to you requesting that you accompany us to Judah and settle there, where you will be safer. Will you consider doing this?"

Isabel looked startled. After a few moments of silence, she slowly answered,

"I must take this to Elohim in prayer and meditate on it. I have always lived here. Such a move is almost more than I can imagine."

"Thank you, mother Isabel. I will await your answer."

"Meanwhile, Hannah, please prepare a good meal for our guests."

"Hannah," spoke up Hanani, "we have food in our baggage. Let us add to the dinner some of our supply."

"Thank you for your thoughtfulness, my Hanani. Now I must prepare the meal."

"I will help you."

"Do you know how to cook?"

"In a very simple way, yes."

As preparations were being made for the dinner, Isabel and Hanani's parents shared some of their family history and values. They found almost instant connections as fellow northerners from nearby towns. They even discovered that they had some distant relatives in common. Speaking with the same northern Hebrew accent helped, also.

The meal was a great success. Amran commented,

"If this is an example of your cooking, Hannah, we welcome you already into our family."

"Thank you, father Amran."

"She is also a good housekeeper and seamstress, father," Hanani added.

"Please," begged Hannah, "enough of your praise. I will become too proud of myself."

"It is all true," Hanani said.

Further discussions with Hannah's family finally convinced them to make the move with Hanani's family. With that decided, all pitched in to help them prepare for the journey. There weren't enough donkeys for their needs, so Hanani accompanied the boys of both families in a search for three more of the little beasts.

"You want how much for this creature?" Hanani asked a merchant. "Why, it couldn't even carry one bag of grain!"

"He may be small, but he's powerful. My price is ridiculously low, but I like your looks and I know these boys."

The haggling continued, with offers and counter-offers. Hanani said at one point,

"Sir, you are nothing but a thief in donkey's clothing!"

"I may be a thief, but I'm an honest thief."

Finally, a compromise amount was agreed upon for the three donkeys. Hanani and the boys left with them, but Hanani noticed the broad smile on the merchant's face. He turned to his young companions and said,

"Well, it appears to me from his grin that we still were robbed. However, I think we got three good ones. What do you think?"

One of Hannah's brothers answered,

"That scoundrel always gets the best of the bargain, but he is the only one in this area who has animals for sale. So, we had to go along with him. Hanani, you did as well as anyone I know in getting him to come down on his price."

"Thank you. I appreciate that."

With all of the donkeys lined up early the next morning, loading them began in earnest.

"Hold still, you flea-bitten refugee from accursed Philistia!" one of the boys shouted. "Do you see this whip? I'll use it on you, if you don't settle down."

A good look at the whip calmed him down. Finally, he and the other donkeys were loaded. Isabel gave a long last look at her home. She had placed it in the hands of friends who would try to sell it. Now she sighed, picked up a shoulder pack and said,

"Let us depart. We gain nothing by standing around here looking at that empty dwelling."

Isabel was helped onto on a padded cart seat to make the journey easier for her. Hanani shouted and the always-contrary donkeys, the flocks and pilgrims began moving toward the south. Their journey was a steady uphill climb into the highlands. Their combined flocks were slow to move. Hannah's mother was still weak, so needed frequent rests. Eventually they approached the new border separating the two sibling countries. Hanani told the group,

"We need to stop here for the remainder of the day and rest. When it is dark, we will cross over. With Elohim's blessing, we should make it safely into Judah."

They located a sheltered site well away from the road and made their simple camp. The women prepared a frugal meal and the boys took turns watching the flocks and the trail from a hidden spot behind some rocks. When it was finally dark Hanani said,

"Let us get back onto the trail, but we must be very quiet. We will go far enough to be safely away from the border and then stop for the remainder of the night."

After slowly traveling in the dark for about an hour, they stopped and again sought out a safe location away from the trail. They found a shallow cave and laid out their bed mats in it after Hanani took up a torch and explored it for any hidden "varmints." The next morning they continued their journey, only to be stopped at a checkpoint by armed guards from Judah.

"Who are you," asked one of the guards, "and what is your business here, strangers?"

"I am a warrior in the king's military force, stationed at Tamar. These are my family and that of my betrothed. We come from the north to escape the idolatry now being practiced there. We seek asylum here in this land that still worships Elohim."

The guards looked them and their goods over and told them to continue, adding,

"May Elohim protect you. Shalom!"

"Shalom," answered Hanani.

They finally arrived at Jerusalem. Only Amran, Rachel and Hanani had been there. Isabel and the children were overwhelmed by the great glistening walls and all of the structures within them. The temple itself, one of the architectural wonders of their world, left them speechless with awe. They had never before seen such a beautiful structure, gleaming brilliantly in the late afternoon sun. Amran insisted on taking a lamb to the priests, to be sacrificed on their behalf. Accompanied by the males in his group, he presented the lamb to a priest, who examined it for any defects and then gave it his approval. As they watched reverently, he intoned a blessing, slit its throat and prepared it for the great altar standing before them. Soon the odor of burning flesh filled the air and smoke drifted slowly upward, curling on itself. The priest then blessed and dismissed them.

"The temple is awesome in its beauty," Isabel commented. "Our great lamented King Solomon made a noble gift, indeed, to our people in building it."

"Yes," Hanani said, "it is beyond description. I pray that it will remain forever as the center of our faith and hope. But now let us seek out an inn, one that has accommodations for our animals as well as for us. We need a night in more comfortable surroundings."

He enquired of a passerby about the location of a reliable inn and was given directions to it. The man's instructions were a bit inaccurate, so they had to seek further guidance from a military officer. He set them on the right street and they were soon at the inn that had been recommended to them.

"Sir," Hanani asked the innkeeper, "do you have a place tonight for two families of weary travelers and their beasts of burden?"

"Yes, I do. Please come with me."

He soon had them and their donkeys settled, arranging feed for the donkeys and flocks, and informing them that food would be brought to them.

"Thank you, sir."

"Have a good night and rest well under the wings of Elohim."

Hanani Turns Smuggler

After their evening meal of the usual flat cakes, a porridge made from crushed grain, cheese, lentils, dried figs, dates and honey, a flagon of wine topped off the repast. Rachel tasted the porridge and commented,

"Humph! Mine is better."

After the meal the adults sat around and discussed where the two families might live. Hanani suggested,

"Consider settling in or near Beersheba. That area is good for grazing and has land on which crops can be raised. The town itself is well protected by high walls and has shops that can supply your needs. And there is ample water from a great well dating from the days of our illustrious ancestor, Abraham. It is called Beersheba—the Well of the Oath—because he and the Philistine leaders made an oath there of mutual peace and protection. In addition, it is not too far from Tamar, so we can be together from time to time."

"Let us look at it," Amran said.

The next day the little band traveled south by southwestward, passing through Bethlehem, Hebron and Debir, en route to Beersheba. It was slow going because of the sheep and Isabel's still-weakened condition, but on the fifth day they arrived at their destination.

Beersheba had a long history. During Solomon's reign it had been upgraded by adding extensive new fortifications. It now was surrounded by a set of sturdy walls. Entering through the first gate they came to, they found the town well planned. Streets were laid out in an oval pattern, paralleling the walls. Amran walked the length of the outermost street and exclaimed,

"This is amazing! Everything is in such precise order. All villages and towns of my acquaintance, except for Megiddo, are haphazard. Even the great capital's living areas were not laid out. They appear to have happened by accident, but this place had a planner."

"I thought you would be impressed," Hanani said. "And did you notice that there are good grazing lands nearby? If you like what you see here, I will return to Tamar and find out if the craftsmen doing reconstruction there are still on the job. If so, perhaps I can convince my commander to let us borrow them long enough to build two adjacent houses for you. You and the boys can be gathering up stones for the foundations and lower courses of the walls. Here is some gold to use for whatever you need to purchase."

"Thank you, son. I will find us temporary quarters, or perhaps we will remain in our tents until your return."

Hanani and Hannah bid each other a fond farewell. Hanani embraced one and all, wishing them safety and happiness until his return.

Tamar

"Shalom!" they all shouted, as Hanani rode off on one of the donkeys en route to Tamar. His mount didn't like the descent down into the crater, but they finally made it safely to more level land traversed by the trade route to Tamar and points east and south.

"Ho, the fortress!" Hanani shouted as he neared the familiar gates. A guard signaled to those inside that Hanani was coming. A glad babble broke out, as they opened the gates and greeted him. They wanted to know everything that had occurred since his departure. Just then Ba'ana walked up. Hanani saluted him and began reviewing his adventures.

"Sir, I took the load of gold ore to the capital, but the new treasurer had no instructions about such a cargo, so didn't accept it. I decided to hurry on north, before he could change his mind. At Megiddo I contracted a goldsmith to melt out the gold, for a price. Then I sought out my family, much to its surprise. Eventually I convinced it to pack up and leave with me.

"Then we went on to Tirzah, where my family met Hannah's family and I had a happy reunion with her. Betrothal arrangements were soon agreed upon. The two families identified quickly with each other. I was finally able to talk Hannah's mother into making the move with us. We obtained more donkeys and set out to the south. We crossed the border at night, but were stopped later by border guards. Once we explained our purpose, they received us with no further complications. We stayed a short time in Jerusalem, where I enjoyed showing them around the city and the temple. Then we traveled on to Beersheba, where they plan to live. And that's the story up to now. Here is the gold I received in Megiddo, minus a small quantity for the two families' expenses connected with the move."

"Welcome back, Hanani," Ba'ana told him. "Do you need any help in getting them settled?"

"Yes, Sir, I do need help. Are your craftsmen still here?"

"Yes, but they are about to leave."

"Would it be possible to send them to Beersheba and ask them to construct two adjacent houses for our families?"

"I think that can be arranged, if they are willing to do so. I imagine you will want to escort them there and get them started."

"Yes, Sir. That would be good."

"Fine. I will talk with them and make the arrangements. I want you to take some of the gold you brought back with you. There will be expenses involved in getting the two families settled."

Hanani Turns Smuggler

One bright, warm morning, as most of them were at Tamar, except in the dead of winter, Hanani led his construction crew out of the fortress and on toward Beersheba, leading three donkeys laden with tools and provisions. Ba'ana sent two other warriors with them, just in case of some incident along the way.

scroll 18

Hanani Has a Shadow

As it turned out, his foresight was fortunate. As the party approached the ascent, Hanani halted the group and said in a low tone,

"Don't look back, but I think we are being followed. Warriors, be prepared. And you craftsmen, have your hand weapons ready, plus any heavy work tool you can manage. I don't know what we face, but I expect it is trouble. For some time now a small force has moved when we moved and stopped when we stopped, staying back far enough, so that we might be fooled into thinking that it is here by mere happenstance. There are some large boulders ahead, right after we take a curve in the trail. They will lose sight of us for a short time. We will send the donkeys on ahead with three workmen, while the rest of us lie in ambush, at least until we know who they are."

The warriors and half of the workmen took up positions behind the boulders. They watched silently until a body of what appeared to be brigands came into sight. Hanani motioned his men to wait until they were almost to them and then to confront them.

"Halt right there, strangers!" he shouted and showed himself briefly. "State your purpose in following us and be quick about it!"

"You will die, Israelite dog!" answered one of their unknown assailants. "You killed my brother."

"And who might that have been?"

"He was a brave Midianite warrior and you killed him in cold blood!"

Hanani Has a Shadow

"No, if it was the incident I think it was, he attacked us and we merely defended ourselves."

"You lie! He was peacefully hunting game and you killed him."

"No such thing. Now back off or suffer the consequences."

"You talk big, little dog. We know you have only workmen with you. They don't know the difference between a spade and a spear. Cut him down, brothers!"

Just then six heads appeared. Arrows flew and hit their targets, with three of the enemy downed. That only slowed them down briefly. Their chief shouted,

"Kill them all!"

Again, arrows flew and this time, stones also, slung by workmen who were skilled in their use.

"Aieee!" screamed the enemy leader. "Die, die, die!"

Hanani knew that if he took out the leader, this little attack would run out of energy in a hurry. So he aimed carefully and shot the leader in the neck, just above his leather armor. He went down shouting blasphemies against Israel and her God.

Just as Hanani had expected, the remaining enemy backed off and then started running away, leaving their dead and wounded.

Hanani took a quick count and found that one of his warriors and one workman had taken arrows, but not in a life-threatening spot. He then checked out the enemy, confiscating their weapons and examining their wounded.

"You will live, you cowards. We will bind up your wounds and send you back from where you came. You are fortunate that I am so generous with you. If it were the other way around, our wounded would have been dispatched without mercy."

They said nothing as their wounds were attended to. Then they were sent on their way, with a little water and bread.

Hanani and his fighters rejoined the donkey train. It was slow going, because of the two wounded men, but they finally made it to the top of the Scorpion Ascent and turned northward toward Beersheba. Arriving there, they sought the town healer, to further attend to the wounded. Hanani told the rest of the men to wait just outside of the walls, as he searched for his and Hannah's families. He found his father and the boys still gathering stones and making mud bricks for their houses. They embraced him fondly. Then one of the boys took him to the women, who were working in their tents.

"Hanani, Hanani, my beloved," screamed Hannah, as she saw him approaching her tent. She embraced him very satisfactorily and then handed him off to the two mothers, who sported wide grins.

"I have brought a team of workmen who will facilitate the construction of your homes," Hanani told them. "We had a little fight on the way here with some Midianite raiders. Two of our men were wounded, but are being cared for by your healer. Now, where do you propose constructing your homes? We need to unload the donkeys and provide them with grain and water."

Amran came up just then and led Hanani to the site for the homes, on two adjacent plots of land just inside the town's outer walls and near the gates.

"Excellent choice, my father," Hanani observed. "This will be handy to the gates, not far from the town well and protected by the walls. Tomorrow I will have our men lay out the dimensions of your homes and start digging the foundations. The boys can all help with this. Now we need to refresh ourselves, eat and get a good night of sleep."

After a meal prepared by the three women, the men all sat around a fire and discussed plans for the work. Finally, as they sought their bed mats, Hanani slipped away to spend a few precious minutes with his beloved.

"Oh how I missed you," he breathed in her ear.

"And I missed you, my wonderful Hanani."

They desired each other, but knew that they could not consummate their love until they were officially wed. To do otherwise would be a scandal, as well as a sin. So they finally tore themselves apart, after a lengthy kiss.

"Sleep well, my beloved," Hanani said softly to her.

"You, too, my hero," she whispered to him.

The next day the workmen soon had the two houses staked out. They were identical in size and form, being in the four-room style. Both houses would share a common sidewall and would have a mutual courtyard at the front, surrounded by a low wall. All of the boys, and even the warriors, worked with a will to dig the foundations. Several men of the town showed up to give a hand, or at least advice, while several women offered to help with the cooking.

Within only a short time, the trenches were ready and the first stones were carefully placed in them. The part of the outer walls that was stone extended about three courses above ground level. On up to the roof, the walls were made of large sundried bricks. The roofs themselves were supported by rough-hewn timbers, over which was laid a generous number of dead tree limbs and palm fronds. All of this was then covered by a thick plaster of mud, reinforced by sand, small stones and gravel.

All that remained to do, after only a few days, was to plaster the walls, to preserve them from the weather, and to make simple furniture. This was soon accomplished. To celebrate, the two families went together to put on a feast for the workmen, Hanani and his fellow warriors. Amran hosted the gathering, beginning it with a prayer:

> Great Elohim, our Elohim, we praise you and thank you for all of your blessings. We thank you for these homes that have been built with such dedication. We thank you for the citizens of this town, who have received us as brothers and sisters. And we thank you for this abundant feast. Bless it and us, as we begin our new life here. So be it.

The betrothal of Hanani and Hannah was old news to the family and folks up north, but had not yet been announced to the people of Beersheba. When Amran revealed this added blessing, all present at the feast shouted their best wishes and went into a celebratory dance in the courtyard.

Two days later Hanani dismissed the workmen with his blessing for a safe journey home and with a bagful of gold for each one. They then left, leading two of the donkeys loaded with their equipment and provisions. Hanani then drew Hannah aside and told her,

"My precious one, I hate to leave you, but I must. It is time to return with my warriors to Tamar. I have been away from there far too much."

"Do you have to go now, beloved?" she asked. "Can't you stay just a day or two more?"

"No, I must leave, but will return at the first possible opportunity."

When the little Tamar contingent prepared to leave, all members of the two families gave them fond farewells, including the other two warriors in their family blessing. Then Hanani hugged his own family and his soon-to-be mother-in-law. He then drew Hannah to him and gave her a kiss she would long remember.

"Shalom, my precious," he said as he turned to leave.

"Shalom in return. Be safe and healthy," she answered.

Hanani was both sad and elated—sad to leave his beloved and his family, but eager to get back to his colleagues at the fortress. What further adventures would await him there?

scroll 19
A New Assignment

"AH, THERE'S THE FORTRESS" Hanani said. "It's good to be back."

"Yes, it is," answered one of his companions, "although I suspect that your heart is more in Beersheba than here."

"You're probably right."

"The three wanderers are back!" the shout went up atop the fortress. Moments later the massive gates creaked open. Hanani and his company were received with joy. Many of their fellow warriors crowded around them, peppering them with questions.

"Hanani, how is your love life going? Is she still going to marry you? "Did you get those houses built, or did they fall down before you could finish?" "Did you bring us back some provisions? We're pretty tired of the same old bread and grain."

"Wait a minute," Hanani said. "Yes, my love life is warmer than ever. She is definitely going to marry me, with the blessings of both of our families. No, I'll have you understand that the two houses are solid, built to last. And yes, we brought you a few items to vary your diet."

"Welcome, then," Ba'ana said, as he sauntered up. "Let's get your animals unpacked and all three of you cleaned up. You smell like your donkeys! Afterward, Hanani, I need to talk with you."

"Yes, Sir. I will be ready within the hour."

Later at Ba'ana's cubicle the commander told him,

"You are to be assigned temporarily to Arad, until a new commander is chosen for there. By the way, Arad is much closer to Beersheba, if that is

A New Assignment

of any interest to you. Then, upon the arrival of a new commander for Arad, you are to return here to assume your new duties as commander. I am to be transferred to Jerusalem. King Rehoboam is fearful that the new Northern Kingdom will breach our borders and attempt to take the capital."

"I am to be commander here?" asked Hanani, incredulous.

"Yes, you are. I recommended you as the most fitting to assume command."

"Thank you, Sir. Are you sure that I am ready for this task?"

"Of course. Otherwise, I would not have submitted your name."

"Very well, Sir. When am I to leave for Arad?"

"Stay here for seven nights. Then you will leave. I will send two warriors with you. Which do you prefer?"

"Let me take Joab and Isma'el."

"Very well. I will inform them."

The week passed rapidly and before they knew it, the time had arrived to leave for Arad. The post all turned out at parade stance, to see them off. Shouts of blessings rang out, as the three went out through the gates and headed again toward the west.

At the end of the third day they arrived at Arad. The fortress was small, about the size of Tamar, but had a village surrounding its complex. The fortress walls were not as strongly built as the one at Tamar, but had the advantage of outer walls surrounding the village. The countryside was a bit more human-friendly than Tamar, with a scattering of trees, pastureland and a small stream. Ba'ana had given Hanani a message of introduction and authorization. He presented it to the commander, Jehud, who received him warmly.

"I will be leaving in a few days. That will give you time to get acquainted and settled in."

"Thank you, Sir. May your transfer go smoothly."

Several days later the commander called his warriors together and bade them farewell. He then left with two warriors and a donkey loaded down with his personal possessions and supplies.

"Shalom!" shouted Jehud, as he left with his escort.

Hanani turned to his new command, saying,

"I will be here only temporarily, but will expect the same obedience and dedication that your departing commander expected of you. You will follow the same roster of assignments. I pray to Elohim for His blessings on your commander and on each of us, as we carry on with our obligations. Understood?"

"Well!" one warrior, evidently the leader of the group, responded, "We do not know you, nor do we know for certain that you have been named interim commander here. Until this is cleared up, we have no intention of obeying your orders."

"What? You doubt my authority? Can anyone here read?"

One warrior reluctantly held up a hand."

"Good," Hanani said. "Now read my orders from my commander and from your commander."

The warrior began to read, but then changed some of the wording as he went along.

"Wait a moment!" Hanani exploded. "That is not what these documents read. You are changing the wording!"

"Your word against his," the leader spoke up.

"What is your name?"

"Matteni."

"Well, Matteni, you seem to be the spokesman for this contingent. Are you aware that at this moment you are risking your life."

"I do not fear you. The entire fortress stands behind me."

"Is this true?"

"Yes," shouted the force.

"Alright, this seems to be a test of authority. Matteni, I challenge you to an archery contest. If you win, my companions and I will leave, but I guarantee that we will return with reinforcements. If I win, on the other hand, you will be imprisoned and all who continue to side with you will be severely punished. Do you accept this challenge?"

"Since I am the best archer here, I have no fear of losing. Let the contest begin."

"Very well. We will each have three arrows. We will shoot them at a target that your men will construct. The first arrows will be shot at thirty paces, the second at sixty and the third at one hundred. The one whose arrows land closest to the center of the target will win. Agreed?"

"Agreed."

The warriors filled a large skin with straw and fastened it securely to a tree. Then Hanani stepped off the distances from which they would shoot, with Matteni verifying each distance. Then they marked their arrows, so that no confusion would follow their shooting as to which arrows were Hanani's and which were Matteni's.

"Matteni, you go first," Hanani said.

"Watch me set this amateur down, men!" he sneered to his companions.

As his cohorts chuckled, he launched his first arrow, which hit near the center of the skin. Then Hanani shot his first arrow, which landed just inside of Matteni's. The same thing happened with the second round. Matteni shouted at him,

"Lucky shots, usurper! Now I will show you how a real archer works."

At 100 paces his arrow landed on the skin, but just barely. Everyone held his breath as Hanani checked the wind, calculated his angle of trajectory, carefully took aim and let his arrow fly. Amazingly, the arrow landed near the very center of the skin, to the joyful shouts of his two companions.

"Matteni, you have been defeated," Hanani told him. "Now you will submit to my authority."

He motioned to his two companions, who took Matteni by his arms and dragged him to a cell at the far end of the fortress. The door was open and a chain was hanging loose by it. They shoved Matteni into the cell and chained the door shut. The entire fortress could hear his cursing, but since he had been bested, the "law" of contest victory sealed Hanani's position as commander. All came up to him and saluted.

"Very well," Hanani said to them, "for one moon cycle you will live on bread and water alone. In addition, you will take 12-hour guard shifts for the entire cycle. Do I make myself clear?"

"Yes, Sir!" they chorused glumly.

"I will take your roster and give you your assignments. Expect them shortly."

Hanani breathed a sigh of relief. His two colleagues congratulated him, not only on his marksmanship, but on his handling of the whole affair.

"Well, I was pretty confident about the first two shots, but not sure at all about the longer one. Elohim must have guided it."

"Elohim or not, it was an amazing shot," commented Joab.

"Thank you. It amazed me, too. I don't think we will have any more trouble with the force here."

Hanani and his friends were only there a few weeks when the new commander, Hezron, arrived with a small guard of warriors. Hanani welcomed him and called the fortress to attention. He presented their new commander and reminded them of the absolute necessity of both respecting and obeying him. Then he escorted the commander to his quarters, telling him,

"When I took command on an interim basis, there was a rebellion against my authority. The ringleader, Matteni, was imprisoned. He remains there for your judgment. The others were punished with a minimal diet and long guard hours for a moon cycle's time. When that period was over, I believed they had learned their lesson well. You should have no difficulty with them, except perhaps with Matteni."

"Thank you, Hanani. You and your two comrades are to remain here for a week, to give me time to get acquainted. Then you may return to Tamar with my blessings. I hear you will be the new commander there, right?"

"Yes, Sir."

"Congratulations. Please help me get settled in and acquainted with my charges here."

"Certainly, Sir."

The seven days passed rapidly. When it came time for the three to leave, the entire squad of warriors, minus Matteni, lined up at attention and expressed their regret at the earlier incident. Then they wished the three well.

"Shalom!" they shouted.

The three warriors answered in kind and set out on their journey.

"Would it be satisfactory with you for us to delay a day or two in Beersheba?"

"I wonder why you would want to do that," Joab laughed, as they turned toward the town.

"Hannah, Hannah!" shouted one of the boys. "Hanani is coming!"

"Are you sure?" she said, as she ran to the door.

He was right. There came Hanani, grinning from ear to ear. He and his two friends entered the house. Out of propriety, he gave Hannah only a brief kiss and hug. Isabel came in and she too got a hug. Then he presented Joab and Isma'el to the family. There was a hubbub of voices, all of them talking at the same time. One of the boys ran next door to tell Hanani's family of his arrival. Moments later they too added to the noise level. Hanani greeted each of them warmly and then said,

A New Assignment

"If I can be heard above this uproar, we are just passing by here en route back to Tamar. For a short time I was the interim commander at Arad. When we get back to Tamar, I am to assume command of the fortress. Commander Ba'ana is being transferred to the capital."

"Commander?" Hannah asked. "Congratulations! I know you will do a good job. When we marry, will we live in the commander's home?"

"Right, my love. I do need to tell you that my time in the military will be extended, due to this change in my status. On the plus side, however, my salary will be increased considerably. Can you live with me for a longer period at Tamar?"

"I will live with you anywhere you go, beloved."

"Thank you for your loving support. And now, all of you boys, I brought each of you a military bow and a set of arrows."

"Great!" they all answered at once.

"For you, dear mothers and sisters, here are necklaces. And for you, father, a military knife of the finest iron. Warning! It is very sharp."

"Thank you, my son. I will handle it with care."

"And now, both mothers and father, would you consider shortening the betrothal period a bit?"

"Well, son, "Amran answered, "I will take it up with the two women. We will have an answer for you before you leave. And what are Hannah's feelings about this?"

"I am ready right now to marry my Hanani!" Hannah exclaimed.

"Now is too soon," her mother said. "Preparations have to be made. Do you agree, Rachel?"

"Certainly. However, now that we live so close together, preparing for the great event will not be difficult."

"Settled, then," Amran said. "We will inform you shortly of the date set for this momentous event."

"Good, father. I will return then with my closest friends for my wedding."

"O Hanani," crooned Hannah. "I can hardly wait!"

"Nor can I, my little dove, but it won't be much longer. Please encourage our parents to settle on an early date."

"Oh, I will, I will."

Two joyful days passed, and then Hanani gave his beloved a lingering goodbye and embraced both families. With that he and his two companions headed back to Tamar. Things were really going smoothly for Hanani, or so he thought. He would soon be wed and would have the added prestige and pay of a commander. What could go wrong at this point? Plenty, as it turned out. There was a serpent among the rocks, coiled and ready to strike.

scroll 20

First Test as Commander

MASSEIAH WAS IMPATIENT. He had inherited military leadership of the Midianites and had received a mandate to seek revenge for their earlier inglorious defeats on Israel and especially, on a warrior called Hanani. One of his spies was a cook in the Tamar fortress, so he had been informed that Hanani was to be the new commander there. The command would change very soon.

"Good!" Masseiah murmured as he read the message his undercover agent had gotten to him. "Before this accursed dog Hanani can settle in as commander, we will strike him."

"And how do you plan to do this, glorious leader?" asked on of his sub-commanders.

"I don't know yet, but it will be a well-planned strategy. I will advise you as soon as I complete it."

Hanani had arrived at the fortress and settled back in, after reporting to Ba'ana on the trip to Arad and Beersheba. The commander then told him that within two days, a transfer-of-authority ceremony would be held. Then, on the third day, he would depart for Jerusalem, taking with him ten of the warriors with the most tenure. He would arrange for ten new men to be sent to Tamar.

"Hanani, it will be your task to further train and incorporate them into your force here. That is always a difficulty, because every change of personnel makes for a new mix of personalities, attitudes and abilities."

"I understand that, Sir, and will proceed with the utmost care."

"I know you will. I wish you the best. You are fully capable of doing an outstanding service here as commander. If you ever need my help or that of my command, do not fail to ask."

"Thank you, Sir. That is reassuring. May I add that it has been a genuine pleasure to serve under you."

"It has been my distinct pleasure to have you under my command."

Two days later the unit was called together, standing at attention as Ba'ana addressed it.

"Brave warriors, you have made my service here quite easy, for which I thank you. You have been dedicated to our great Elohim, to your king and to me. I know you will continue in the same way under your new commander, Hanani. He will assume the leadership as of now. I pass on to him my seal and insignia, as well as my sword. I will be taking ten of you with me and will send ten others to fill the vacancies. May Elohim's blessing rest on each of you."

"Shalom, Commander," Hanani responded for the group. "We will all miss you. Warriors, a salute and battle shout for our commander."

The warriors shook the walls of the fortress with their loud shout, "Great is El Shaddai! The battle belongs to Him!"

Ba'ana then mounted a donkey and led his departing warriors out of the fortress and onto the road to the Scorpion Ascent.

Hanani signaled the gates to be closed and told his warriors to proceed with their new schedule of watches and other assignments. They would have to do double duty until their reinforcements arrived and were trained.

"Well, that went smoothly, don't you think?" Hanani asked his new adjutant, Joab.

"Yes, it did. Now it is back to routine."

Part of the routine was Hanani's move into the commander's home. He had few possessions, so accomplished the transfer in short order. He looked around it and said,

"This place is too empty. I can hardly wait until Hannah arrives as my wife."

First Test as Commander

Several days passed quietly. Then a night guard reported that he had seen one of the cooks slip over a wall right after dark and drop down to the ground by rope.

"I didn't know what he was up to, Sir!" he reported to Hanani. "But I thought it strange. Why would he be slipping out at night? There is nothing around here to do."

"Good job, warrior. Let us arrange a little reception for him when he returns. We will hide three men by the top of the rope. When he climbs over the wall, they will capture him and bring him to me."

Two hours later the guards nabbed the errant cook and led him by force to Hanani.

"So, you were up to no good out there," Hanani said sternly. "Just what were you doing?"

"N . . . n . . . nothing, Sir."

"Nothing, in the middle of the night. I think not. Again, what were you up to?"

"I . . . I was meeting a girl?"

"A girl? There are no girls in this area. Quit lying!"

"I was delivering a message to a friend."

"Who is this friend and what was the message."

"That is confidential, Sir."

"So confidential that you climbed down over the wall to deliver it?"

"Yes, that is right."

"What was in that message?"

"I cannot tell you, Sir."

"Cannot or will not? Guards, I guess we will have to convince him to tell us the truth. Call out the men. We will run him through the gauntlet over and over, until he decides to cooperate."

"Yes, Sir!!!" they chorused, as they headed off to call the warriors from their sleep. When they staggered out, Hanani explained the situation. That got their attention. They went to get their swords and returned to form two facing rows.

"Now, cook, you will run the gauntlet until you drop from exhaustion. If you are still not willing to speak up, you will rest briefly and then run it again, and again, and again. Begin running!"

The prisoner ran as fast as he could between the two rows, with each warrior slapping him hard with the flat of his sword. This went on and on, until finally he cracked.

Tamar

"I give up, I give up," he panted. "I was delivering a message to the leader of the Midianites about the fortress, its manpower, its weaknesses and your command."

"So you are a spy for the Midianites! That must mean that you are a Midianite, yourself."

"No, I am your brother. The Midianites ordered me to betray you. You see, they knew I was married to a Midianite girl and said they would deal harshly with her and her family, if I did not cooperate. Don't you see? I had no choice."

"You could have reported this to me at the very beginning."

"I didn't think you could help."

"I think we could have helped, had we known. But regardless, what are we to do with you? You are a traitor and a spy."

"Please be merciful to me. I was under great pressure to do what they said."

"I could order you executed, but instead, will confine you to the prison cell for a moon cycle. Then you will be shackled each day and forced to dig a well until you reach water. Pray that water will show up in a few days. Otherwise, you will spend a long time in that dark well."

"Thank you, Sir, for sparing my life."

"Guards, take him to the cell and chain him."

As they escorted the prisoner away, Hanani told his warriors,

"Back to bed for what is left of the night. You may have been a little too gleeful in exacting the punishment. Just remember that your turn to be chastised may come one day. All not on guard duty may sleep an extra two hours in the morning. Dismissed!"

As they walked away, Joab strode with Hanani to his home. He commented,

"Well, Hanani, you passed your first test as a commander in fine style. I appreciate your restraint and fairness."

"Why, thank you, Joab! Coming from you, that is high praise."

Hanani returned to his lonely house and Joab returned to his quarters in the fortress.

Masseiah called his junior leaders together, saying,

First Test as Commander

"The word we had from our spy was only fair, but he reports that the fortress is down to only twenty warriors. That mangy dog Hanani is still new at the game of commanding, so I think it is time to attack them. I am concerned about one thing, though. Suddenly there are no more reports from our "mole." If he was caught, he may have told all. That makes our job more difficult, because it robs us of the element of surprise. But we can mount a much superior force and can overwhelm that puny fortress. Agreed?'

"Yes, noble leader. Whatever you say!"

"Quit your flattery! Can we, or can we not, capture Tamar and kill that demon Hanani?"

"It is as you say, great leader. We have a much superior force."

"Very well. During the next moonless night, five days from now, we will be in position around the fortress and will attack at dawn. Prepare your weapons and supplies. Make sure the camels are fed and watered. Be ready to leave at dawn."

"Yes, Leader!" they answered.

Hanani's force made special preparations for the reception of their unwelcome "guests." They had an ample supply of arrows, stones for slings and even large stones for the catapult. They also had several pots of oil kept hot, burning coals and straw to wrap around arrows and turn them into flaming torches.

"I want six of our best archers to hide out near the probable route of the Midianites. After they pass you, follow them and when you are sure of your shots, fell several of them taking up the rear. Disappear again quickly, before they even know what has happened. Then again follow them, repeating your performance. Continue doing this until they are near the fortress or until near daylight. Hide out again and await developments. If you are needed to attack them from the rear, I will wave a white cloth. Then charge quickly and do as much damage as you can. At the same time we will intensify our repelling of their forces. Your task is dangerous, but vital to our success. May Elohim protect you. Now go!"

The gate was shut and Hanani's force made ready for the assault. That night passed quietly, with only the mournful sounds of some nocturnal bird breaking the silence. To its cry came answering cries from others of its flock. When, near daybreak, the birds abruptly stopped their singing, Hanani signaled his defenders to be ready. They ran silently to their positions on the wall. Then the chilling battle cry of the Midianites echoed off the fortress walls.

"Here they come!" shouted Hanani. "Make every shot count. Lookout, how many?"

"I estimate almost 200, Sir!"

"Good odds. They have 200. We have El Shaddai fighting for us. That puts us in the majority!"

From the fortress they could see the enemy running toward them, carrying scaling ladders.

"When they get near with the ladders, dump oil on them, followed by flaming arrows. That should set the ladders on fire. While they are trying to put out the flames, take them down."

Hanani's team rained arrows, stones and hot oil on the invaders. They even fired off large stones from the catapult. This slowed down the attackers, but then they regrouped and charged ahead again.

"Hmmm!" Hanani said. "I guess they have not learned their lesson yet."

Even as he said this, the sky darkened ominously. Lightning flashed, thunder rolled, heavy rain fell and hail the size of sling stones began to strike the ground. This was an extremely uncharacteristic event for a region that seldom saw even rain.

"Protect yourselves with your shields!" shouted Hanani. "I told you we were in the majority."

The Midianites were in a panic, breaking their battle line and running for any shelter they could find. Shelter was almost nonexistent, so they continued to run pell-mell toward their camels, some of them falling from the impact of the hailstones on them and all of them dropping their weapons. When they got to where their camels had been tethered, no camels were to be seen. They had ripped up their tether stakes and fled, frightened by the storm.

Finally, the storm let up, but not their problems. Just then six warriors appeared, ordering them to concede defeat.

"No way, pigs!" Masseiah shouted.

"You will concede!" said Hanani in a steely voice. He and most of the fortress's defenders had come upon the Midianites from behind, with their weapons ready to use.

All but Masseiah raised their arms in surrender. He cursed them and told them to stand their ground.

First Test as Commander

"How can we? We have no weapons," one of his aides answered.

"Then use your fists!" he cried.

"Fists against arrows and stones? We think not."

Masseiah pulled out his knife and lunged at his aide, only to be pinned to the ground with a lance Hanani threw with deadly aim.

"Now, if the rest of you don't want the same medicine, I suggest you march back to the fortress. There we will strip you of everything except your tunics and headgear. After that, some of us will escort you in chains to Jerusalem, where you will become slaves of our great king. I'm sure he can put such adventurers as you to good use. Joab, select a detail and prepare to leave as soon as possible for the capital. Rations for our prisoners will be minimal."

Turning to his command he said,

"Be very vigilant. The Midianites will come looking for their vanished brothers. We wouldn't want to be ungracious hosts if they show up. Apparently, not one of you was even scratched. I'm proud of you. Let us praise our great Lord for giving us the victory. Joab, I'm sending with you a letter of commendation for our entire unit. Perhaps King Rehoboam will see fit to reward our warriors in some way. Whether he does or not, he will know that they conducted themselves valiantly. Now, dismissed. Warriors, store your weapons and prepare to take up your normal duties. Things should be quiet for awhile now."

Within the hour Joab and his guard led the shackled prisoners out the gate and toward the Ascent.

"Go with Elohim!" the troop shouted to them as they left.

One day Isma'el asked Hanani,

"Brother, you are restless. What troubles you?"

"Nothing of any great import," Hanani said.

"Nothing? It must be something. You pace back and forth. You eat little. Come on. Tell me!"

scroll 21

Hanani Takes a Bride

"Well, it is Hannah," he explained. I miss her so much and wish she were here to share my life."

"So, it is a restless heart, is it? That can be remedied. I know that Joab is your closest friend. He is the logical one to act as your emissary. When he returns from the capital, why not send him on another and much more agreeable errand?"

"Isma'el, you are right. With Elohim's blessing, we will act on this right after Joab returns. He will enjoy being the arbitrator in this matter."

After a few more days Joab and his fellow warriors arrived. They had hardly entered the fortress until Isma'el told Joab that Hanani had an urgent matter for him to solve.

"Oh? What is it? Is something wrong?"

"Nothing wrong. He will explain."

Joab reported in to Hanani, who asked him,

"Welcome back, my friend. How did it go? Were there any problems on the way?"

"Not really, Hanani, unless you consider that all of our captives hated us with a passion."

"That is understandable. Were there any difficulties in delivering them to the authorities?"

"Not any, especially after I explained the situation and gave them your message. Now, what is on your mind?"

Hanani Takes a Bride

"I have decided that I wish to marry Hannah now and wait no longer. I need for you to go to Beersheba as the groom's friend and start making arrangements. Are you willing to do this?"

"Of course. I will leave on the morrow."

"Thank you, my friend. Go with Elohim and may He bless your journey and quest."

Early the next morning Joab was on his way with two companions. They made quick time up the Ascent and on to Beersheba. Following Hanani's directions, they were able to find Hannah's home easily. Shouting a greeting from the gate that opened onto the courtyard shared by the two families, they were soon admitted. They asked for Hannah and she appeared. Recognizing Joab, she gave him a warm welcome. He then introduced his two companions.

"What is your mission here?" she asked Joab. "Is Hanani ill, wounded or in some other difficulty that I need to know about?"

"Yes," chuckled Joab, "he has heart trouble. He misses you terribly and has sent me to make arrangements for the two of you to wed just as soon as possible."

"Mother!" Hannah called. "We have a very important message from Hanani."

Isabel appeared, a bit flustered by the sudden appearance of three men in their home.

"Yes, my daughter. What is this message that has required the presence of three men to deliver it?"

"May I explain?" asked Joab. "I am here to ask you to begin preparations for a wedding feast. Hanani wants to marry your daughter just as soon as possible."

"Oh! He doesn't want to wait any longer?"

"No, honored mother. He is lonely, especially now that he lives by himself in the commander's house. More precisely, he is lonely for your daughter. Will you give your permission for us to proceed with the wedding plans?"

Turning to Hannah, she asked,

"Daughter, are you willing to move ahead now with your wedding, rather than waiting?"

"Oh, yes, yes, yes!"

"Then that is settled, except for bringing Hanani's family into this change of circumstances. Hannah, go fetch his parents, please."

Hannah lifted her skirt and ran across to the next house, shouting,

"Amran, Rachel, are you there?"

"What is it, dear Hannah?" asked Rachel.

"Mother has asked both of you to come over to our house right now, if you can."

"My husband is out in the fields, but one of the boys will call him. We will be there in a few moments."

Hanani's parents received the news readily, expecting that this eventuality might happen sooner, rather than later. They agreed without any hesitation to the change. Amran then asked,

"And when will this great wedding feast occur?"

"Joab spoke up, suggesting,

"Will one complete moon cycle be sufficient time for preparation?"

The two women exchanged glances and nodded. Isabel told Joab,

"That gives us very little time, but we can manage it. Go and bring Hanani to us in one more moon cycle."

"Very well, mother of Hannah. I will return there on the morrow and we will proceed as you suggest. Thank you, all of you, for making my quest so successful."

Arriving back at Tamar without incident, the three entered the fortress and called out for Hanani, who ran up to them and asked, without any greetings,

"Well, what did they say? Did they agree?"

"Yes, my friend. They agreed. I am to escort you to Beersheba at the end of one more moon cycle. Then we will celebrate together your wedding feast."

"Thank you so much, Joab. I knew I could count on you. However, you will not celebrate every detail of the wedding with us. No one, not even you, will enter the bridal chamber."

"Not? How selfish of you!"

Both laughed and began thinking together about their journey back to Beersheba. Hanani would need a special military uniform for the great event. He sent a message with a passing caravan en route to Jerusalem. It was to be delivered, along with a payment in gold, to the official military seamstress. Her instructions were to make a splendid uniform for a commander about to be wed. One of his other uniforms was sent as a pattern. She would have ten days in which to do this. She would deliver the uniform to the fortress commander, to be sent with new recruits for the Tamar fortress. He calculated that they should be leaving in sufficient time to get the uniform to him.

Hanani Takes a Bride

Things hummed along in the two adjacent homes. Earlier, Hanani had left with them a quantity of gold as his wedding mohar. They used it to stock up on the food and wine they would need, as well as cloth for a special white gown Hannah would wear. As the moon cycle came toward an end, all was pretty well ready. Word had gotten out to the whole town and to military friends at Arad and Araor. The three oldest boys from the two families had already been dispatched to Tirzah and Megiddo, advising relatives and friends of the upcoming wedding.

All that remained to do now was to prepare food for the feast, which would last for seven days. Large quantities of flat cakes, roasted grains, dates, figs, nuts, vegetables, melons and wine were stored up. Lambs would be killed and roasted just before the feast began.

Amran erected a huppah in the center of the courtyard, which had been swept clean. Friends of the two families gathered up wild flowers, herbs and spices for the event. One family even brought a basket of dried Damascus fruit, a real delicacy. Another brought honey. Yet others brought jewelry for the bride, perfumes or gifts for Hannah's new home.

Finally the day arrived for Hanani to appear. He did so on schedule, riding a white horse borrowed from Jerusalem and dressed in a splendid uniform. Joab and three other warriors were riding mules. Each was garbed in his dress parade uniform.

Joab went on ahead and announced in his best military voice,

"Behold, the bridegroom comes!"

Everyone ran out to greet Hanani—everyone except Hannah. She was cloistered in a room in her home, joined there by ten virgin friends, as was the custom.

"Hanani, how splendid you look!" his mother said to him.

"He certainly does!" added Isabel. "He is a very fit mate for my daughter."

Hanani dismounted, hugged the two mothers and led his colleagues to a hitching post for their mounts. They took down their bags and sat on benches in the shade of trees near the houses. Hanani took out a small leather pouch, which he presented to Isabel.

"Mother Isabel, here is a special wedding gift for Hannah to wear during the feast. Would you take it to her?"

"Gladly, my son."

"Oh, mother," Hannah asked her when she entered the inner room, "How does my Hanani look? Is he as handsome as ever?"

"More so, my daughter. You will be very proud of him. Now, here is a gift he has sent to you."

"What is it?"

"I don't know. Why don't you find out?"

She opened the pouch with eager hands, to reveal a sparkling golden tiara.

"Ohhh!" she exclaimed. "It is so beautiful!"

"It will look good, along with intertwined flowers, on your lustrous hair."

"Oh, Mother, you flatter me too much."

"It isn't flattery, my daughter. You are beautiful both inside and out. I am so proud of you."

As the time passed, guests began to arrive from far and wide. Commanders from other fortresses, even as far away as Jerusalem, came. Family members arrived from the north. The entire city of Beersheba came out en masse. Suddenly the courtyard, both houses and even the narrow stone street in front were crowded with people.

That evening the first of the series of banquets was spread. Hundreds of guests milled about, awaiting the signal to greet the bride and begin the feast. Finally came the shout from Joab,

"The bridegroom is coming! Bring out the bride!"

Hannah walked slowly out of the house into the courtyard, accompanied by her friends. Even with her face covered by a thin veil, she drew a gasp from the assembled guests. She was positively radiant, from her glistening tiara to her shiny white sandals. She walked slowly to the huppah, where she sat on a bench bedecked with flowers. Then her friends went over to a waiting Hanani and escorted him to the bench. He lifted the veil from Hannah's face, took her hands in his, and, quoting from love stories, he sang to her.

"How beautiful you are, my beloved, how beautiful!" he crooned. "Your lips are like two anemones. Your hair is black like the mane of a prancing warhorse! Your cheeks are as rosy as a sunset. You are beautiful beyond comparison!"

"My handsome husband!" she responded. "How manly you are! Draw me after you where you will."

Seeds were now thrown to the ground in front of the couple, an old fertility rite. A vase of scent was broken, its fragrance filling the area. Then the couple stood before two small vials. They stomped on them, shattering them as a sign of two individuals no longer two, but one. A local priest then read from the Torah about the sanctity of marriage, intoned a blessing from the ancient Scripture and presented the couple to the assembled guests, who shouted blessings, suggestions (some ribald) and best wishes.

Hanani and Hannah then disappeared into a room especially prepared for them. They turned to each other in awe.

"My precious lamb," Hanani said to her, "I love you so much."

"And I love you equally, my hero. But isn't it time now to stop talking and take some action?"

"I'm shocked by your brazen behavior!" laughed Hanani, as he drew her to him. Their kisses became longer and more urgent. Finally, they disrobed each other and gazed longingly at the body of their beloved. They then lay down on a couch and consummated their marriage. Hanani was tender and considerate of his bride's virginity. Coached earlier by the two mothers, she, in turn, responded slowly but eagerly to his advances. Their first time to be together intimately lacked some finesse, but that would come.

"O my wonderful husband!" Hannah sighed. "You are the perfect lover."

"Perfect? How do you know this, since I'm the first man to take you like this?"

"I just know."

"And I know that you are the most perfect bride in the world."

"And may I ask how you know this?"

"As you said, 'I just know.'"

The feast continued unabated for several more days, until finally the wine ran out. Then the guests began to wander away, but only after again wishing Elohim's richest blessings on the couple.

Shortly afterward, Hanani gathered their parents together and told them it was time for him and his bride to leave.

"Must you go so soon?" asked Isabel.

"I am the fortress commander. It is time for me to return to my duties. Hannah, can you be ready to leave by morning?"

"Yes, my husband. I will be ready."

"Good. My dear father, mother and new mother, we will not be that far away. Come to see us. We promise to visit you from time to time."

The next morning Hanani, Hannah, Joab and the other two warriors were packed up and ready to leave. Hanani had arranged for a covered cart to carry Hannah and their goods.

"Farewell, our daughter," said the parents. "May you be as blessed as was your namesake, the other Hannah. We will miss you terribly."

"Farewell, my parents and family. I too will miss you."

Amran then led them in a blessing and the little caravan started off along the street to the eastern gate.

scroll 22

Tamar Stricken

IT WASN'T MUCH OF a honeymoon—no inn, no celebratory food, no privacy. It was just that tedious journey down the Scorpion Ascent and across the wilderness to the fortress. Hanani apologized frequently to his bride, but she told him,

"Do not fret over it, my husband. We will soon have time to ourselves."

"I pray that we will. I want you in my arms."

"I, too, my beloved."

They all breathed a sigh of relief when Tamar finally came into view. It even looked good to the men after their absence. Hanani greeted the guards and the gates came creaking open.

"Well, Sir, did you wed in style?" asked one of the warriors.

"Ask Joab or Hannah. I was too enamored with my bride to remember much of what happened."

"Sir," the warrior chuckled, "I imagine you remember some of it."

"Well . . . maybe some," he admitted with a grin.

Isma'el came up just then and greeted the newly arrived party.

"Welcome, Hannah, to our humble fortress. And Joab, just how did the marriage feast go?"

"Splendidly!" he answered. "Hannah was radiant, the food was excellent, the wedding party was congenial and only a few got drunk on the wine."

"Hannah, what do you say?"

"What do I say? I say it was the best wedding feast I have ever attended."

"Of course, but you are a bit prejudiced."

Everyone laughed heartily and then several proceeded to unload the beasts and take them to water. Hannah indicated which items were to go directly to the commander's home and which were to remain in the fortress. Soon everything was arranged to her satisfaction.

"Isma'el," Hanani asked, "Do you have anything extraordinary to report in my absence."

"No. Everything was calm. A pride of lions attempted to attack our goats, but we drove them off."

"Good. My thanks to you for manning the fortress during my journey. Now, if all of you will excuse us, I need to spend some time with my bride."

"I imagine you do," laughed Isma'el.

Hanani grasped Hannah's hand and they skipped out through the gate and to their nearby home. Entering it, they found that the warriors had cleaned it fairly well, not to Hannah's standards, but well, considering their lack of expertise in the art of housekeeping.

"What do you want to do first?" asked Hanani.

"If you will draw some water in the corner bathing basin, I will take a bath and prepare myself properly for my husband. Would you like to join me?"

"Would I? Need you even ask?"

Soon the two were bathing each other and then kissing and embracing. Hannah got out and dried herself off. Then she applied fragrant ointments to her body, while Hanani watched her every move. She then whispered,

"Don't just sit there in the basin, my love. Come and I will dry you off and rub you down with this oil."

He was out of the basin instantly and happily submitted to her ministrations. When she was through she walked slowly to a bed mat and lay down on it. She motioned for him to join her, which he eagerly did.

We will not invade their privacy further, except to say that they experienced the next best thing to Heaven itself.

"My precious. My dove. I love you so much!" Hanani whispered.

"I love you even more, my great lover. Now our honeymoon has really begun. You will not have to hurry back into the fortress, will you?"

"Yes, but not until tomorrow, or maybe the next day."

"Wonderful. Now, you must be hungry, after all of this exercise. I will get up and prepare us something."

Tamar Stricken

They prepared together their meal, interspersed with hugs and kisses. Afterward they ate and cleaned up everything, Finally, they fell asleep in each other's arms, most content with their new life.

On the third morning Hanani tore himself away from his lover's arms, dressed and returned to the fortress.

"I'm happy to see you finally came up for air," Joab said to him.

"It was tough duty, but someone had to do it. Any news to report?"

"Only this. One of the warriors was suddenly stricken with some ailment that has laid him out."

"What kind of ailment?" asked Hanani.

"We don't know. Come and take a look. Perhaps you can determine what it is."

Hanani found the warrior deathly ill. He was drenched in perspiration, and very hot to the touch.

"Has he drunk water from some other location than our spring?" he asked the warrior who had accompanied him.

"He has not, as far as we know."

"I don't know what this sickness is. We need a healer, but none is nearby. There is one in Beersheba. I will ask Joab to go there and bring him back. He can take two horses."

Joab was soon on his way to Beersheba, galloping away in a cloud of dust. After he had left, Hanani told Hannah about the ill warrior. She offered to attend him and would not take no for an answer.

"I know something of healing. A woman's touch can often be of help. I will keep his perspiration wiped off and make sure he stays warm. Has he had frequent liquid passing from his bowels? If so, I will mix up some herbs that will help alleviate that problem. Hanani, bring me oil and wine. I will mix them and anoint his body."

"I will bring them. And yes, his bowels have moved frequently and they are liquid."

"I suspect that he has a flux caused by something he ate or drank. But in case his illness is something that can spread to others, let us isolate him."

"Yes, my physician wife. I'm worried about something, though. What if he passes his malady on to you?"

"That is a chance I must take, dear husband. Let us pray to Elohim for guidance and protection."

The days passed slowly, with the patient showing only slight improvement. Meanwhile, several others were stricken and were moved to the separate area in which the first had been placed. Hannah had her hands more than full, attempting to care for the very ill warriors, now numbering six. So far she had escaped this "plague," but knew that it might be only a matter of time until she came down with it, too.

Finally the healer from Beersheba arrived with Joab. He was a man of good bearing, grey-headed but strong of mind and body, whom both Hannah and Hanani had met. He carried with him a large leather bag which contained extra clothing and various instruments and potions. Hanani explained to him,

"Thank you so much for coming, honored healer. Here is the situation. First, we had one warrior down with some kind of serious ailment. Soon afterward, another five were stricken. We have isolated them from the rest of our command. Hannah has been attending them, keeping their perspiration washed off and anointing them with a mixture of oil and wine. Since they have runny bowels, she has given them a concoction of herbs. This has helped them some, but they are still in serious condition."

"Your wife has done well," he answered. "Take me to your sick men."

"This way, Sir."

After examining each man, the physician asked,

"What fruit have they been eating?"

"We recently got in a supply of fresh Damascus fruit. The men have all enjoyed eating it."

"So," replied the healer, "that may be the answer. We don't know why, but in warm climates such as ours, consumption of some fresh fruits can cause these very symptoms."

"And what is the cure, Sir?"

"First, all of the remaining fruit must be boiled. Then, those who are ill and others who may become ill are to be given a mixture of herbs that I will leave with you. Two times a day they must consume a cup of the mixture, liquefied by boiling it in water. After about a week they should show improvement. Then they must rest for at least another week before resuming their duties."

"Very well, Sir. We will follow strictly your orders. Now, what do we owe you for your services?"

"No charge for men serving our country. However, you may reimburse me for the medications, provide me with a week's worth of food and send an escort with me back to Beersheba."

"That is very generous of you. When you arrive back home, please greet our two families for me and Hannah."

"I will be happy to do so."

The healer spent that night at the fortress. The next morning he looked in on the patients, congratulated Hannah on her service to them and, in company of Isma'el, left for home, well laden with food and a generous tip.

"Now, Joab," Hanani said, "it is a matter of following the physician's orders and waiting for our colleagues to recover."

Fortunately, no other individuals became ill, not even Hannah. However, they were not yet safe.

scroll 23

An Attack Foiled

THE STRICKEN WARRIORS WERE still on their mats. Hannah continued to attend them. They embarrassed her with their words of gratitude for helping them improve.

"I only did what I could," she answered.

"No," spoke up one. "You did far more than that. You even endangered your health and life. We will never forget your care for us, right?"

"Right" the others chorused.

She had just turned away from them when a shout rang out from the tower.

"Ho, the commander! Warriors approaching and they are not ours!"

Hanani rushed out of his cubicle and asked,

"How many?"

"I estimate at least 200 to 250."

"Well, we cannot hope to overcome that many, with some of our warriors down and Isma'el gone. Joab, what if we tried a different strategy? What if we opened the gates and invited them in?"

"What?!" answered Joab, shocked.

"We will bandage up our ill warriors, darken their faces and around their eyes and tell them to moan and groan convincingly. We will ask the chief of that bunch to visit our comrades and tell him that they have some horrible disease. Since they are still perspiring, he should be convinced. Let us watch his reaction."

"Brilliant! You have been around Commander Ba'ana. I can tell."

An Attack Foiled

"Proceed with this little ruse immediately. Meanwhile, I will greet our 'visitors' and ask them what they want."

Hanani climbed to the wall and shouted,

"Ho, unexpected guests. What seek you?"

"You are all to lay down your arms and surrender to us," answered the chief of the enemy force, a band of Amalekites. "If you do not, we will take down your puny fortress, stone by stone, and kill all of you."

"You won't need to do that. We will open our gates to you."

The gates creaked open and the enemy stormed in.

"Before we surrender, Sir, I would like for you to visit our ill. Several are down with a dread disease. Come and see. You may be able to suggest a cure."

"What kind of dread disease?" the Amalekite chief asked.

"We don't know, Sir. I'm not sure that you should risk staying here."

"Since I think you are stalling, I will see for myself. Lead me to them and be quick about it."

"Very well, Sir. Come this way."

The chief called two of his aides and the three followed Hanani. They entered the isolation area and were greeted with the proper moans and groans. The enemy chief looked long and hard at them, felt the forehead of one and then bolted out of there. Running to his band, he ordered them to leave immediately.

"Hurry!" he shouted. "Let us get away from here. The commander was right. The fortress is consumed by some kind of terrible malady."

Once well away from the fortress, he ordered a halt. Then he washed his hands carefully and poured wine over them, hoping to free himself of anything that might have infected him. He broke into a sweat and cried out,

"I have their disease. Find a nearby cave or oasis and leave me there with some food and drink. Go on back without me. Someone come back in a week to see if I am dead or alive. Now go!"

His band needed no other command. They raced to their staked-out camels, hoisted him onto one and before long found a small oasis, where they left him. The dust from their galloping beasts was all that remained behind.

"Well, that worked wonders, didn't it?" Hanani asked Hannah and Joab, who were nearby.

"My husband," Hannah crooned. "You are blessed of Elohim."

"I agree," added Joab. "That was a stroke of pure genius. Not an arrow flew. Not a stone was slung. Not a warrior was wounded. They came in quickly and just as quickly fled."

"I suspect they are still fleeing," Hanani chuckled.

Flee they did, all the way back to their camp. When they reported what had happened and how they had left their leader at an oasis, the tribal chiefs huddled together for a few minutes and then announced,

"You are not welcome here. You may be carrying that plague with you. Leave here immediately."

"But where, honored elders?"

"We do not care where. Just get out of here. After a moon cycle's time, if none of you is down with this plague, you may return, but not before then."

"Yes, honored elders."

Several days later Isma'el returned and ten new warriors arrived, to replace the ten who had left with Ba'ana. Hanani welcomed these new members of his contingent by ordering a parade appearance of his entire force. The troops formed a quadrangle around him as he spoke.

"Welcome to Tamar. I am Hanani, your commander. You will be required to integrate quickly into our routine. We will test your ability with the bow, sword, sling and lance. Once that is completed, anyone who does not measure up well will expect to undergo rigorous training, until you do measure up. All of our lives depend on your ability with your weapons. You will each be placed into the rotation for day and night guard duty. Anyone guilty of insubordination, dereliction of duty, sleeping during your watch or other violation of our regulations will be punished severely. Do you understand?"

An Attack Foiled

"Yes, commander," the ten answered.

"Good. You will find me a fair commander, who expects even more of himself than of you. You will find that I am quick to praise, but, when necessary, also quick to accuse. My adjutant Joab will show you to your quarters. Dismissed."

"What do you think, Isma'el?" he asked. "Do they look like capable and dependable reinforcements?"

"I don't know, Hanani. We will have a better evaluation of them after a week or two."

"I'm sure of that. I want you and Joab to organize their testing and training."

"It will be our pleasure," Isma'el answered.

The new warriors were soon trained and took their place with little difficulty in the Tamar force. Hanani was content. The fortress was well organized. Food was adequate. All were in good health and spirits. Well, there was some griping about the heat of the area and the sameness of fortress life, but that was to be expected. All warriors complained at times. It was part of being in the military.

And Hanani's home life? It was wonderful! Hannah was a constant joy to him. Whatever she did, she did well. Hanani came to work each morning almost walking on the clouds, if there had been any. He knew, however, that something untoward could happen at any time, just as it had in the past.

scroll 24

Elohim's Hand on the Enemy

THAT SOMETHING UNTOWARD HAPPENED soon. It came as a shock to Hanani and the longer-term warriors, bringing them back to reality. One day the tower man shouted,

"A force of warriors approaches from the south! And they are not ours."

Hanani rushed up the stairs to the top of the wall. He soon concluded that they were Midianites. Apparently they had not learned their lesson earlier and were back for more teaching.

"Warriors!" he shouted. "Every man to the walls, with full armament and weapons. Joab, slip out through the Needle's Eye and bring Hannah here for safety. Isma'el, arm the catapult. Cooks, bring up as much hot oil as you can. Elohim, watch over your servants here at Tamar. Give us courage to face this determined enemy."

The Midianite force stopped and one figure strode forward briskly. He raised his voice in a taunt for the defenders.

"I am Masseiah, whom you thought you killed, you swine, Hanani. I recovered and am now here to kill you. I hereby challenge you to individual combat to the death. If I kill you, all of your flea-bitten dogs will become my slaves. And your little bride—yes, I know about her—will become my concubine. If you win, which you won't, we will become your slaves. Do you accept my challenge and its terms?"

"You give me no choice. I should have finished you off when I had the opportunity. So now I must see to that unfinished business. Give me time to put on more combat armor and take up my weapons. Then I will meet you in the center of the fortress. Your men will wait outside."

"No, my men will wait inside. I want them to witness your defeat and beheading."

"Very well. They may come in, but must lay their arms down in a heap just inside the gates. I have no intention of permitting you to signal one of them to pin me to the wall with his lance. Now, what weapons shall we use?"

"Lance and sword. I am a master at both."

"Well, so am I. I will return in a moment and then let the contest begin!"

"My Hanani, I am so frightened," sobbed Hannah, as she ran to him. "What if he kills you?"

"Do not fear for me, beloved. I have no intention of being killed, not with our wonderful future before us. The man boasts too much. Our great Elohim will deflate his boasting."

"Please be very careful."

"I will. Now help me put on my armor."

Moments later Hanani walked out into the fortress's central court. He faced Masseiah and prayed aloud to El Shaddai. Masseiah ridiculed him, lifted his eyes to the heavens and cursed Hanani's God.

"You, El Shaddai or Elohim, whatever you are called, are nothing, a nobody, a god no one has ever seen! Do you hear me, little god? My sword is stronger than your arm. I will soon dispatch your lackey and prove it!"

He then spat on the ground and shouted,

"Come, spawn of the devil! Soon I will feed your carcass to the wild dogs."

"You have blasphemed my Lord. He will not allow you to live."

"Your god is a weakling! I have no fear of him."

Everyone stood deathly still. Hanani stepped back three paces and stood on guard. Masseiah took that as a sign of cowardice, so charged forward, lifting his lance high to throw it.

But suddenly he stopped in midstride, grasped his chest with a loud grunt and fell in a heap on the ground. His aides rushed over and checked his pulse. They looked up, shock etched on their faces. Their leader was dead without a lance being thrown or a sword being drawn. Their entire force backed up against the walls, petrified with fear. Hanani reminded them,

"As I said moments ago, Elohim does not allow blasphemers to live long. In this case your leader's punishment came surely and swiftly. You will now surrender to us. By the terms of Masseiah's challenge, you will become our slaves. I cannot use you here, so you will be taken to Jerusalem, where you will serve our great king for life. You will not attempt to escape, for that would be contrary to the terms your leader laid down for our combat. Joab, arrange a party to escort our prisoners to the king. Before you leave, however, we must forge chains for our distinguished captives. Meanwhile, tie them up here in the courtyard and post a guard over them."

"Very well. We will be ready soon to depart."

"O Hanani," Hannah sobbed. You are so brave and Elohim is so powerful!"

"I wasn't all that brave, dear wife. I was shaking inside, but I did trust in Elohim to care for me and punish my enemy. He did both in a powerful way, for which we are all grateful."

"I still think you were very brave. You, dear husband, are my hero."

"I hope you will think that all of our life together."

With that Hanani dismissed his warriors to their tasks and headed home with his wife.

The Midianite camp, set up at an oasis some 20 leagues from Tamar, was a welter of tents, baggage, some sheep and goats, and a few camels left over from those taken on the raid. Palm trees gave some shade to the area. Grass was green near a bubbling spring and its adjoining pond, in stark contrast to the surrounding barren plateau.

Concern for Masseiah set in among the camp guards and clan elders, as he and his warriors failed to return.

"What could have happened?" asked Hakkoz, who had been left in charge. He called the elders and asked them what they thought.

"Should we go in search of them or continue to wait here?"

One old greybeard answered,

"Masseiah is perfectly capable of defending himself and he has a large force of battle-hardened warriors with him. They must be busy loading up loot from the fortress. I suggest we wait until the morrow before we worry too much about them."

"Very well, we will wait."

Elohim's Hand on the Enemy

They all then turned to their tents and the evening meal being prepared for them. Hakkoz ate in silence, a sense of foreboding wrapping both his mind and body in a blanket of gloom.

After a restless night, he was up at dawn. He searched the area and then climbed a nearby hillock, to see if the missing party was arriving. He saw nothing except more plateaus and low hills— no telltale column of dust that would signal the return of a large party of camels and riders. Calling the elders together, he proposed that most of them go in search of their war party.

"Do you agree?" he asked.

"Yes," they chorused. "You will lead a party and the younger of us will accompany you. Some must remain here to tend our flocks and keep watch over our tents and possessions."

"We will leave by the third hour," Hakkoz answered. "Who will go with me?"

Several offered to go and began making preparations for departure. Soon they were on their way, a dozen old men in search of their party of young warriors. Their train of aged, scruffy camels didn't exactly run. They shuffled along, complaining in camel fashion at being forced to carry their human loads.

Arriving finally at Tamar, they requested an audience with the commander. Hanani signaled for the gate to be opened and they plodded in. Descending from his mount, Hakkoz explained their mission.

"Honorable commander, we have come to enquire about a raiding party that left our camp several days ago and hasn't been seen since. Do you know anything about it?"

"Yes, Ancient One, I do. The raiders arrived here and were admitted into our fortress. Their leader, Masseiah, challenged me to an individual contest, the winner taking all of the enemies captive and confiscating their possessions and animals. He blasphemed our God and was struck down miraculously before he could deliver one throw of his lance. His companions were taken prisoner and are already being escorted in chains to Jerusalem, where they will be servants of our great king. Since we had no need for their camels, you will find them tethered at a nearby oasis. You may take them and return in peace to your people. We were saddened by the whole affair and understand your dismay. Now go, but first, do you need water or food for your return?"

"Thank you for your report. We trust that you buried Masseiah properly?"

Tamar

"Yes, we did. Again, do you need anything for your return journey?"

"No, commander, but accept our gratitude for your thoughtfulness. If one of your guards will lead us to our camels, we will be leaving."

"Shalom."

"We will go in peace, young upstart!" Hakkoz muttered as they exited the fortress. "But we will be back to take out our revenge on you!"

"Do you suppose they have learned their lesson, or will they be back?" Joab asked Hanani.

"Of course they will be back, and with a very large force. Midianites never forget, nor do they forgive, so we must remain vigilant at all times."

scroll 25

Boundary Dispute

THE EDOMITES WERE STILL seething over their defeat at Sela, which was supposedly impregnable. Now their agents in Jerusalem reported to them that large quantities of gold were appearing in the city, shipped from the Tamar region. Where in the Tamar region? Were the Israelites mining this gold on Edomite territory? If so, they were nothing but common thieves, robbing the rightful owners of their wealth.

"What shall we do about this?" asked Gesham, the military commander of the much-depleted Edomite forces. "Do we not investigate and if the gold is from our domain, must we not secure the area from further mining by those greedy Israelite dogs?"

His adjutant answered, "Certainly we must find out. If the gold is ours, we must demand that all of it mined until now be returned to us and all future mining be stopped until we can take the mine over."

"I agree, but would add one more thought: If the mine turns out to be in their territory, we need to find a way to move our boundary markers to include the mine and to confiscate their gold ore."

"Excellent, Sir."

"Alright then, let us plan a way to verify the location of the mine, then, if necessary, move the boundary markers to make the mine our property. In addition, we will raid the donkey trains carrying the ore to the fortress or afterward, en route to Jerusalem. Is that understood?"

"Certainly!"

Soon, just to be on the safe side, Gesham ordered a crew to locate the mine and then move at night the boundary makers between Judah and Edom, placing them beyond the mine entrance. When that was accomplished, he and a party of his officers appeared at Tamar's gates, demanding an audience with the commander. Hanani appeared and motioned for them to be admitted. Gesham wasted no words getting to his point. He pointed a finger at Hanani and shouted,

"You mangy thief! You are stealing our gold from right under our noses. Now, upon pain of death, you will return all of your ill-gotten gold to us and you will do this immediately."

"What are you talking about? We are mining gold from our own national territory. We verified this by locating the boundary stones which were some 500 paces toward the rising sun from the mine's location."

"You lie, young upstart commander, and we will prove it. Come with me and we will locate those markers, which are well toward the setting sun from the mine."

"Very well. I will bring an escort with me and we will see about this matter."

He motioned to Joab to round up six warriors and accompany him. Arriving at the first boundary marker, they found it to be, as Gesham had said, toward the setting sun from the mine."

"Wait just a moment!" exclaimed Hanani. "This stone has been moved. See those footprints leading from where it was to where it is now. We will lift the stone and take a look under it. Aha! There is a small prickly plant under it. The stone has not been there long or the plant would have died. So, who is the liar now?"

"Idiots!" Gesham spat out at his staff. "Didn't you order your men to erase their footprints? And you didn't even think to have all signs of life erased from under the stone."

"So, this is an admission of your trickery. Go back where you came from, now! Any more such attempts will mean your death."

"You haven't heard the end of this, commander. We still have some other tricks at our disposal."

"I'm sure you do Now, however, we are forewarned to be prepared for them."

As the Edomite chief and his followers stalked off, Hanani said to his staff,

Boundary Dispute

"What else will they try? I suspect attempts at raiding the fortress, or raiding our donkey trains carrying the ore to Jerusalem. We will need to have plenty of guards for the trains. Once the ore has arrived at Jerusalem, they will not be able to intercept it. When is the next ore shipment to leave?"

"In about three days," Joab answered.

"Then, let us send a contingent of 12 warriors with it and move it out at night. By daybreak it should be well on the way. But, just to be safe, let us send out in daylight a dummy train, manned by two or three men, with only debris from our earlier rebuilding in the bags the donkeys are carrying. To protect it, we will send a contingent of warriors, but they will be far enough back so as not appear to be a part of the train. If they are needed, a signal will be arranged to alert them."

Both trains left on schedule. Edomite raiders took the bait and followed the second train. Seeing them coming, one of the train handlers warbled a signal. Catching up with the party, their leader said,

"You, scum, if you value your lives, take those bags off of the donkeys and be quick about it!"

"Yes, we will do as you say."

The bags were soon off of the donkeys. The raider chief opened one, to find nothing but scraps of stone and wood. He then opened the second, third and the rest. He exploded,

"What kind of trick is this? Where is the gold?"

"What gold?" asked one of the donkey handlers, a warrior in disguise. "We have no gold."

"Then where is it?"

"Well beyond your reach by now!"

"You are all dead, you miserable curs."

"I don't think so. Look behind you."

He glanced back over his shoulder to see a well-armed force with lances and swords drawn. Then the donkey leaders pulled off their robes to reveal their uniforms and weapons. The raider knew he had been outdone, so ordered his men to lay down their arms. They were then bound and marched back to Tamar. Hanani told them harshly,

"So, Edomites, you have been defeated at your own game. Now go back home and report in. I think your punishment there will be sufficient to teach you a lesson. If not, come back and we will see to your proper education."

Tamar

The raiders slinked out of the fortress minus their weapons, knowing they would face severe punishment at home for their failure.

The couple had just finished a very satisfactory meal, when Hannah said to her man.

"Hanani, be prepared! I have something important to say to you."

"Oh, and what is this important announcement, my love?"

scroll 26

An Unexpected Recall

HANNAH EXPLAINED SHYLY,
"You are going to be a father!"
"I what? A father? Does this mean you are to have a baby?"
"To be so very bright, my husband, sometimes you are very dense. Yes, I am with child."
"Are you alright? Is there something I need to do?"
"You need to continue to love and care for me. Also, you need to go fetch my mother as the time approaches. I want her here with me for this great event."
"Certainly. But meanwhile, you need to take care of yourself. I don't want you to do any heavy physical work."
"My dear, I am not suddenly a palace princess. I have worked most of my life. Only as time draws near will I need to do less strenuous work."
"We're going to have a baby!" Hanani shouted, as he ran to the fortress. "We're going to have a baby!"
Everyone quickly gathered around him, offering congratulations, as if he were the one to give birth.
"Which do you want, a son or a daughter?" Isma'el asked.
"A son, of course, but if it is a daughter, I will care for her and love her, just as I love her mother."
"Well said, brother!" Isma'el answered.
Hannah suffered the usual nausea and other discomforts of early pregnancy. She could not even endure the smell of food cooking, so Hanani

brought her food from the fortress. They weren't exactly gourmet meals, but sufficed.

"Well, if our commander hasn't turned into a household servant!" his warriors ribbed him. "Are you also keeping house over there in your 'palace,'" one of them asked.

"Yes, I am," Hanani answered good-naturedly. "I may grow too domesticated to care for any labor around the fortress. That will mean that you will have to do all of it."

Momentous things were happening, however, that would yank Hanani out of his domestic chores.

Sheshonk, Libyan ruler over Egypt, wished to aid his ally, Jeroboam, who had sought refuge with him during the reign of Solomon and had subsequently become ruler of the new northern kingdom of Israel. Jeroboam longed to recapture the southern kingdom of Rehoboam and reunite the entire region. Not only that, but Sheshonk had designs on Rehoboam's Judah. It was located in a pivotal position between Egypt and the eastern lands. If he could secure Judah and, already having Israel under his influence, he could sweep northward without any real obstacles in his way.

"Mnkere," he said to his military commander, "I plan to mount a campaign against Judah. We must proceed with the largest force we have ever assembled. Our very presence there in such numbers will turn the blood of the inept sheep of that little kingdom to water."

"Very well, great God Sheshonk," the pharaoh's commander-in-chief answered. "And how soon are we to embark on this conquest?"

"I want us to be under way by the next full moon, understood?"

"So close, noble Sheshonk? How can we possibly be ready to march on such short notice?"

"You shall be ready. Is that clear?"

"Yes, my Lord. It will be done as you ordered."

An Unexpected Recall

Rehoboam angrily paced back and forth in his strategy room, holding a scroll he had received from Egypt. He grumbled,

"Who does this Sheshonk think he is, threatening me? I am Elohim's appointed ruler and he is a nobody, a Libyan nobody, who usurped the throne of Egypt. Now he has designs on my country and my throne, the very throne of David. Advisors, where is he now and how large a force does he have?"

"Sire," said Abijah, his son, "reports are that he is on the Way of the Sea with 1,200 chariots, 60,000 horsemen and countless foot warriors."

"That cannot be true. Who has been feeding you lies? Sheshonk does not have anything like those numbers."

"I am sorry, my lord. Our watchmen have been observing and counting. They are like a horde of grasshoppers. How can we possibly stop them?"

"We must! Elohim will fight for us."

One of his advisors, Seraiah, reminded him,

"Sire, the prophets have warned us that, since many of our people have rejected Elohim, to worship the gods of the land, Elohim himself has rejected us. If that is so, we cannot hope to win out against Sheshonk."

"I do not wish to hear such cowardly and traitorous talk, Seraiah. Our cities have been well fortified and our capital is nearly impregnable. The Libyan will wear out his warriors as they beat their heads against the stout walls of our cities and fortresses. Now summon our own valiant warriors from all of our fortresses, leaving only a small number in each. I especially want their commanders to come and help us defend our city against these heathens."

"Very well, Sire," Seraiah sighed. "This will be done immediately."

"Alright, then. All of you are dismissed. I want to plan our strategy."

Seraiah and Abijah hurried off to carry out the king's command. Soon couriers were on their way to the scattered fortresses of Judah.

"Commander! Commander!" the gatekeeper shouted. "You have a message from our king."

Hanani hurried to the gate, thanked the courier who had just arrived and asked him to remain overnight, in case an answer was required. He then sat down and read the message:

> Rehoboam, son of the great Solomon and ruler of Judah and Benjamin, to the commanders of the king's fortresses, greetings. We have been invaded by a very large force from Egypt, led by Sheshonk, the Libyan ruler. I therefore order you to come to our defense in Jerusalem. Bring half of your warriors with you. This must be done immediately. You are to send me a return message with the number of warriors you will provide and the projected date of your arrival. This is of the utmost urgency.

"Great Elohim!" gasped Hanani. "This is grave indeed! Joab and Isma'el, to my command center."

When they had entered, he explained the situation.

"Do we know how many men Sheshonk has and how soon he will arrive at Jerusalem?" Joab asked.

"All I know is that it is a very large force. We are required to send immediately to the king half of our force here and I am to lead it. We must be prepared to leave at first light. Select the men to accompany me. Meanwhile, you will serve as interim commander here. Isma'el, you will be my second-in-command. Gather up the supplies we will need in transit and prepare all of our weapons. Understood? Fine, then. We have very little time. I must explain this to Hannah. She will not be happy about it, but we have no choice. Joab, I want you to send a runner to Beersheba and bring her mother here to care for her in my absence.

"Yes, Hanani. I will see to it."

It was a tearful goodbye in Hanani's home, as he left his expectant wife for an unknown fate. He explained,

"This is an order from our king and I cannot ignore it, as much as I would like to do so. I hate very much to leave you, but you can see that I have no choice. Meanwhile, I'm sending for your mother, to care for you and keep you company while I'm gone."

"Thank you, my husband. I will miss you so much! If you can, bring me back a new robe. Mine is too heavy for this place, except in the cold season. Oh yes, the garrison is out of salt and so are we. And please, please be careful, for our sakes and that of our future little one! Now don't be looking at all of the palace concubines!"

"I will miss you, too, and I will be very careful. Don't worry about the concubines. I will not look at them much."

"What do you mean, much? I don't want you looking at them at all."

"My precious one, they pale in comparison to you."

"Flattery will get you somewhere, my husband. Now give me an unforgettable farewell.

After a last long kiss and embrace, Hanani walked over to the fortress, where he was joined by 25 warriors, led by Isma'el.
"Are we ready?" he asked.
"Yes, Sir!" they chorused.
"Then let us get on our way. Carry on, Joab, and shalom!"
"Shalom!" Joab answered, as the two embraced.
Moments later they headed out through the gates. Hanani gave a salute to Hannah, as she stood in her doorway watching them leave.
"Dear Elohim, please guard her and keep her safe. If I'm delayed, may she deliver the child without difficulty," he prayed.
"O Elohim, protect him and his troop. Bring him back safely to us," she prayed. "I couldn't bear to live without him, nor could our unborn child."
Dismaying events were about to unfold in Jerusalem, soon after Hanani and his force arrived there.

scroll 27

The Battle for Holy Ground

Hanani and his force arrived in Jerusalem in record time. Hot and tired, they were received by none other than Ba'ana, their old commander. He welcomed them warmly and assigned them to quarters, instructing them,

"After you are cleaned up, rested, and have a meal, I will bring you up to date."

"Thank you, Sir," Hanani said. "It will be a pleasure to serve under you again."

Shortly later Hanani was in Ba'ana's command center.

"Sit down, Hanani," he told his young friend. "Tell me about your life at Tamar."

"Well, Hannah and I are married and are expecting our first child."

"Congratulations! And how is your command?"

"Joab is in command in my absence. Both he and Ishma'el are excellent officers and should one day have commands of their own."

"Very good. I will keep that in mind. Now, for our situation here. It is not at all good. Sheshonk is on the way here with myriads of warriors and hundreds of horsemen and chariots. Our only hope is in El Shaddai, our great God of battle."

"What provisions have you made for defense of the city?"

"We have further fortified the gates and walls where we found them weak, filled to capacity all of the pools in the city and stocked up a large quantity of grain and other foods. We have made extra weapons and have checked our catapults. All is as ready as we can make it."

The Battle for Holy Ground

"Sounds very thorough to me. I don't think the enemy will attempt to breach the walls or gates on the Kidron Valley side. The approaches there are too steep for easy access. The gates near the temple and palace are the more likely points of attack."

"You are right in your assessment, so we will concentrate most of our warriors along those parts of the walls. All we can do now is wait and pray."

"Great God Sheshonk, we have taken down all of the more important fortified cities to the west of Jerusalem," Mnkere reported. "Soon we will arrive at the capital of this perverse people."

"None too soon. I am already tired of this expedition," Sheshonk sighed.

The shout went up that Jerusalem had been sighted.

"We will halt here atop these hills and organize our command center. Then we will prepare for our siege of the city," Mnkere shouted to his staff. "You will disperse our forces according to the plan we have worked out."

Soon the ponderous troop made up of Egyptians, Libyans and Cushites, came to a halt. Upon orders from their commanders, units took up positions all around the city. They then erected a luxurious pavilion for the Pharaoh atop the Mount of Olives. From there he could see the entire city and all of his military forces. His headquarters, supported by wooden poles and enclosed by colorful linens, sported multiple carpets on the ground and great silken cushions for lounging and sleeping. His portable throne was covered in gold, with carved lions at its sides and a crimson carpet leading to it. Slaves stood ready to do his every bidding.

Beyond the royal pavilion military leaders put up a protective ring of tents. Down on lower hills and in valleys nearer the city were the tents of the lesser officers, horsemen and charioteers. The common warriors had to be content with a mat on the ground. The countless horses were staked out across the hills surrounding the city. Battering rams and catapults were positioned near the gates of the city. This made for an imposing military array, indeed. Hanani, standing by Ba'ana and other commanders, drew in his breath and exclaimed,

"I have never seen such an army in my life. Who can stand before it?"

"As I said," Ba'ana answered, "only our el Shaddai can. We can do little by ourselves to stop that swarm of hostile bees about to sting us."

147

All was quiet for several days, as the defenders became more and more anxious. Then, early one morning, came a thunderous shout from thousands of voices. The entire area around the city seemed to quake under the tread of warriors and noise of chariots. Siege machines were rolled up and the first wave of the battle for Jerusalem began.

Those who got too close to the walls paid with their lives, as expert archers and slingers downed them. But they were few in comparison to the myriads behind them and were trampled on by horses and chariots.

"Stand fast for El Shaddai!" shouted the commanders on the walls. "He will fight for us!"

Wave after wave of enemy forces attacked the city, especially along the northwestern corner, exactly where Hanani had thought they would concentrate their attack. Day after day they pressed their charge, but with little effect. Only the loss of thousands of their warriors, felled by the accurate shots of archers and slingers along the walls, kept them from pressing their attack.

"What is taking so long?" demanded Sheshonk after many days of futile effort. "Use our siege weapons. That is why we dragged them so far."

"Yes, great Pharaoh," Mnkere answered. "We will do that immediately."

The ponderous siege machines were rolled into place, at the cost of many more enemy warriors. Finally, they began to batter against the gates along the northeastern walls.

"Thump! Thump! Thump!" the jarring hammering of the machines beat against the gates. Day after day and week after week the gates and walls shook with the battering they were taking. It shattered the nerves of all of those inside the walls.

"O Elohim," the people prayed. "Save us from this horde of Egyptians."

No answer came . . . no cessation of the interminable banging.

"Why have we not yet broken the gates?" demanded Sheshonk in a loud and angry voice. "What is this puny city? How can it withstand our machines?"

"Great Sheshonk, they must have reinforced greatly their gates and walls."

"By the gods, no gate can stop me! Redouble your efforts, day and night. I want at least one gate down by the morrow. Understood?

The Battle for Holy Ground

"Yes, Great Lord Sheshonk. It shall be done."

"It had better be, or you will be done, permanently!"

So the battery against the gates continued day and night. Finally, after weeks of effort and the loss of more thousands of the enemy, the Old Gate was hammered down with a loud crash and hordes of warriors entered the city with a bloodcurdling shout of victory.

Ba'ana rushed toward the breach, calling for reinforcements. Hanani responded with his warriors, as did other commanders with their troops. They downed hundreds of enemy warriors, but thousands more poured in.

Then Ba'ana, who was at the front of the defending force, was struck with several arrows.

"Ba'ana!" Hanani shouted, as he rushed to the side of his fallen friend. "Ba'ana, can you hear me? O Elohim, spare his life. We need him so much!"

But his prayer was to no avail. Ba'ana was wrapped in the silent shroud of death. Hanani cradled his hero's head in his arms and wept. Preoccupied with the loss of his mentor, he didn't notice an enemy slipping up behind him. Soon he was knocked cold with a mace and was dragged away, to be chained as an animal. He remained unconscious for hours, missing the horror that was going on inside the city.

"Very good!" Sheshonk exclaimed. "Our warriors are in the city at last! Mnkere, order our men to pillage their temple and palace, along with the homes of their wealthy. Take all of the gold, silver, gods and other items of any great value. Do not burn the city. I want it preserved as a puppet capital for my empire. Any likely-looking warrior commanders will be taken as slaves. Kill the remainder, but leave the noncombatants."

"Yes, Great Lord Sheshonk. It will be done as you ordered."

Several bloody hours later Mnkere reported to the pharaoh,

"Noble God Sheshonk, we have done precisely as you ordered. Booty is being collected in a great mound outside the city. We found some small household idols, but in their golden temple, strangely enough, we found no gods at all, only some altars, a great golden lamp stand and a large gold-plated box containing nothing of value to us. In the king's palace we located a number of gold shields, which we have carried off. We also took from there jewelry and other costly items. Our men are still going from house to house in the wealthy quarter, searching for valuables."

"Good. Now bring me their king. I wish to see him prostrate himself before me and pledge me servitude. And hurry. I want us away from this accursed place and back in our blessed land!"

"Yes, Noble Pharaoh."

Mnkere obeyed his master to the letter, knowing that if he failed, he would be banished, enslaved or executed. He personally went down from the mount and into the city, where he located Rehoboam, hiding in a closet of his palace. Using an interpreter, Mnkere announced,

"You, little king of this insignificant country, are hereby ordered to appear before the Great Pharaoh Sheshonk, Lord of the Two Lands and Sovereign over the Earth. You will accompany me now in my chariot."

"Well, I have no choice, since you have invaded our land and captured our holy city."

"You have no choice whatsoever. Get up and follow me now!"

The chariot horses labored up the steep incline to the Mount of Olives. Arriving there, Mnkere motioned Rehoboam to remain in the chariot while he entered the Pharaoh's pavilion and announced the arrival of the vanquished king. Moments later he emerged and motioned Rehoboam to enter, warning him to prostrate himself before the Great Pharaoh.

Again Rehoboam had no choice. He entered deferentially and prostrated himself before the pharaoh, resplendent in his war crown of the Two Lands, his golden chains, rich robe and scepter.

"Alright, puppet king, arise" Sheshonk ordered him through his interpreter. "Henceforth you are my vassal and will do my bidding in all things. I have spared your city, but any attempt at rebellion will be met with the total destruction of not only your city, but your land as well. Is this understood?"

"Perfectly, Pharaoh."

"I will assign a minister of state to dwell in a suitable home in the city. You will provide him and his family and staff with provisions and financial support. You will also pay into our royal coffers the sum of 50,000 pieces of gold annually, as well as shipping to us a fifth of all of your produce, flocks and herds. In addition, you will provide warriors on demand. These requirements will be spelled out in a scroll, with both my sign and yours affixed to it. That is all. See that you complete it fully. If you fail, the consequences will be disastrous. Now, return to your little kingdom and rebuild it."

"Yes, Pharaoh. We will do as you require."

The Battle for Holy Ground

But where was Hanani in all of this? Was he an enemy commander, treated with at least a small amount of respect? Was he merely a slave? Where was he and how was he faring?

scroll 28
Oh, My Hanani!

"Hannah, Hannah, I have bad news for you," a Tamar warrior sadly told her, out of breath and bedraggled from a long, long run. "Commander Hanani fell in the siege of Jerusalem and was taken captive. I don't know what has become of him."

"My Hanani . . . captured? How?"

"I don't know, my lady. I heard that he had been captured. We are thinking that he has been taken to Egypt, but we don't know what his fate will be there."

"Thank you for bringing me this news, sad as it is. Won't you come in a refresh yourself?"

"No, my lady. You will want to be alone with your grief and I can clean up in the fortress. Shalom."

"Shalom, warrior. Thank you again."

Hannah slowly turned toward her door and entered, where she found her sister Jemimah holding her infant son. One look at Hannah and Jemimah knew that the news was bad.

"What is wrong, my sister?" she asked.

"Hanani was captured in Jerusalem and has disappeared. They think he may be in Egypt, but no one knows for sure where he is and what his fate may be."

"I'm so sorry!" Jemimah told her. "But let us go to Adonai in prayer. If He so wills, our Hanani will be returned to us, or at least be kept alive."

Oh, My Hanani!

Following their prayer for Hanani's safety, Hannah went to her sleeping mat, where she prostrated herself and wept her misery. She was still there when a delegation of warriors, led by the interim commander, Joab, came. Jemimah let them in and called Hannah. Wiping her face, she joined them.

"Our lady, we are so sorry about our commander, your husband. We stand ready to do all we can to help and console you. Both of you please consider eating your meals with us. Now, let us pray with you."

"Certainly, and thank you."

"Great Adonai," Joab intoned, "may your beneficent hand hover over our commander, Hanani. May he be brought back to us, if this be your will. Comfort our beloved lady, Hannah, as she mourns the loss, at least temporarily, of her husband. Amen."

As the contingent turned to leave, Hannah thanked them for their concern and promised to call upon them for any need she had.

As she watched them return to the fortress, she said to Jemimah,

"Sister, we must make the best we can of the situation, for Hanani's sake and that of the baby. This will mean an additional burden on both of us, but we will just have to bear it."

Days turned into weeks, with no word at all from Hanani. What were the two of them to do? Should they stay there at the fortress, or should they return to Beersheba and the embrace of their family?"

"Jemimah," Hannah said one morning, "don't you think it is about time to move back home? A new commander will show up one of these days and will want this dwelling. Or perhaps Joab will be named commander. At any rate, we need to think about moving."

"I agree with you. Perhaps we should wait a few more days and then ask Joab if he can arrange for a wagon and escort, to accompany us home."

"Yes, I will approach him about this. Should we prepare to move in about a week?"

"Yes, it won't take us long to prepare."

Hannah continued her ardent prayers, with tears, for Hanani's return to them. Was he lost to them for all time?

scroll 29

Prisoners of War

THE TRAIN STRETCHED OUT for a day's journey, as jubilant Egyptian, Libyan and Cushite warriors chanted their victory songs. Camels and donkeys were loaded down with the spoils of Judah and Jerusalem. Their route took them down eastward to the Way of the Sea and from there to distant Egypt. At the front rode Sheshonk in his special chariot, gold-plated and covered with a bright awning. His personal advisors and officers rode horseback or in chariots, forming a protective square around his godlike presence. Far back, following the host of warriors and the captured animals, shackled near-naked prisoners shuffled along, breathing in the dust of the huge mob and the many animals in front of them. The captives numbered about fifty, most of them Rehoboam's personal military staff and fortress commanders.

Among these was Hanani. Each dragging step took him farther and farther from his beloved. He felt within reason that he might never again see her or meet his child. He knew for a fact that his hero, Ba'ana, was dead. He wondered and prayed about Isma'el, since he had not seen him since the Old Gate caved in.

"O Elohim, my Lord, why? Why Ba'ana? Why the sacking of our great city and profaning of our sacred temple? Why am I being taken to Egypt as a slave, perhaps never to be with my family again? I am far from the hero that our ancestor Joseph was, when he overcame all obstacles of slavery and unjust imprisonment to become an important minister under the Pharaoh.

"No, I do not have his stature, but I pray for courage to face what lies ahead, just as he did. And I pray for the chance to escape and flee back to

Prisoners of War

Tamar. I place my life and that of my beloved Hannah in your hands, O Elohim, my Strength and my Redeemer . . . "

The endless trek continued through unbearable heat and choking sand. Twice a day the prisoners were given a few swallows of water and a loaf of stale flat bread. When they complained, their guards answered sharply,

"Shut up, Israelite dogs, or you will receive no food or water at all!"

They were not allowed to stop, even for a call from nature, until the entire troop stopped. As evening fell, the troop halted for the night. The prisoners, chained to trees or chariots, could only slump over and try to get some sleep.

Babustis rose out of the northeastern Delta region as an imposing array of palaces, temples and the administrative center of the Libyan 22nd Dynasty. It was surrounded by verdant fields of grains, fruits and vegetables. Palms and fruit trees abounded in the rich alluvial soil. The Delta was blessed with many mouths of the Nile, as it coursed toward the Great Sea. Babustis was located on the Tanitic mouth and so had a constant supply of water.

For the arriving warriors and their pharaoh, Babustis was a welcome sight. Heralds had gone on ahead to announce their coming. As they entered the gates, Sheshonk led the way in his resplendent war chariot, pulled by matching white horses.

"Make way for our great Pharaoh Sheshonk, Lord of the Earth, and his victorious army!" the Pharaoh's bodyguard shouted. Crowds quickly prostrated themselves before their "god" to cheer the victorious military force. Behind him rode his generals and officials. Following them were camels and donkeys bearing the vast amount of booty taken from Jerusalem and other cities of Judah. Then came the hordes of warriors, grouped by units and led by their commanders. They were followed by thousands of captured cattle. Except for a rear guard, the chained prisoners were last in line and shuffled in, exhausted and half starved. Yet, they held their heads high, to indicate that they may have been captured, but were not broken in spirit.

155

"Elohim, I don't understand why you have brought us here as slaves," cried Hanani. "Yet, not as we wish, but as you wish. May your holy will be done through us. May your grace allow us to return to our people."

The captives were led quickly to a fortress, where they were released from their chains, cleaned up and given simple servants' garb. A bath felt so good! Then they were placed in a barracks. Their guards pointed to thin, dirty and bug-infested bed mats, indicating that they were to sleep. After all they had been through, they needed no persuasion.

"How can we escape from here," Commander Zattu from the fortress at Arad asked? Several had ideas, none of which seemed to hold much chance of success. Finally, Hanani spoke up,

"After we are separated and assigned to different officials, there will be little chance for us to escape as a unit. If we want to try to flee as a group, we have very little time. If, on the other hand, we try individually to escape, some of us perhaps can manage to escape, but probably not all."

Three days later the prisoners were marched to a camp to the east of Babustis, where the official over their guards explained through an interpreter that they were to remain until assigned their duties under new masters. They had slogged through endless marshlands, splashed through small canals, fought their way through cane and papyrus growths, and attempted to slap away hordes of mosquitoes. The heat was oppressive, but the humidity made it even worse. Sweat poured down their faces and into their eyes. It was total misery to these men from the hill country, but didn't seem to bother their guards at all. Once at the camp, they were placed in a large tent under minimal guard.

Hanani took stock of their situation and said to his fellow prisoners,

"We may never have a better opportunity to escape than now. They must think we wouldn't try anything, since we are out in the middle of the marshland. Our guards are few and with care, they could be overcome. When and how should we prepare our escape?"

"First," Zattu said, "Hanani is correct about our chances at this point. Second, we should attempt our escape at night. And third, we should scatter out in small groups, heading in different directions. That will make it much more difficult to recapture us."

"I agree," answered Elon, commander at Beersheba. "Or perhaps we should all head toward the heart of the Delta and then split up. Our captors would never expect us to flee farther into their country."

"Very good," Hanani said. "I think your idea has real merit, agreed? Now, how can we overcome our guards?"

"Why not take down one tent pole and break it into pieces?" another of the captives asked. "We can use the pieces to club our guards."

"Might work," mused Hanani, "if they don't notice in the dark that it is gone. Does anyone else have a suggestion?"

"How about disconnecting some tent ropes and make nooses out of them?" asked Elon.

"That might be less noticeable. Are we all in favor? One problem, though. How can we cut the ropes?"

"I saw a sharp rock in the fire pit," someone offered. "As soon as it is dark and the guards are not watching, I will slip out and get it."

"Good!" answered Hanani.

scroll 30

Nothing but Sand

NIGHT FELL AS SILENTLY on the marshland as the flight of a bat. When it was quite dark, the prisoner who had offered slipped out of the tent, slithering silently and slowly along the ground. Picking up the stone, he reversed his course, stopping every little way to blend in with the dark surface of the soggy ground. Finally he entered the tent and showed his trophy—a stone that had been fractured, leaving a jagged edge.

Soon the captives were cutting through the ropes, making lengths of a strong cubit each. These were then tied as a noose large enough to slip easily over a head and then pulled tightly around the neck.

"We will also need cords for tying up the guards," Hanani said. "My count of them is ten, so let's make enough cords for that purpose. I see no reason for killing them. If we get away, their fate will be sealed by their superiors."

When all was ready, the prisoners slipped by twos out of the tent, each armed with a noose and a length of cord. Zattu said he would sound the cry of a night bird as a signal to attack.

Moments later came a mournful "Hooo, hooo, hi." The prisoners jumped their guards, most of whom were asleep, dead drunk. They soon had them trussed up and tied to tent poles. The guards were shouting what appeared to be obscenities, but the captives could not understand the words. They gave a fond wave of the hand to the guards and raced westward, taking what few weapons they could find.

After running for some distance and sloshing through papyrus-choked muddy swamps, they stopped to catch their breath.

Nothing but Sand

"The more swamps the better!" Hanani said to the other escapees. "They won't be able to follow our tracks through all of that muck."

"Man, I haven't run this far since my training days," complained one of his companions. "How much farther are we going to head west before we double back?"

"This may be far enough," answered Zattu. "What do you think, Hanani?"

"I agree. Let's split up into parties of eight or ten and turn eastward, but not on the same track. Let's sound off by numbers through six."

When the groups were divided out they worded a joint prayer for safety and then agreed to meet at the far northeastern corner of the Delta adjacent to the sea. They gave each other a heartfelt "shalom" and then turned eastward, but some distance apart.

"You let all of them get away, those miserable dogs?" asked an incredible Egyptian officer. "And they had no weapons! How could this happen?"

"We do not know, Sire. They jumped us in the middle of the night and soon had us trussed up."

"You will find them and bring them back or you and your fellow guards will be executed for your folly. Is that clear?'

"Yes, Sire. We will find them. You can count on that!"

"If you value your miserable hides, you will recapture them. Now get on with it."

"Yes, Sire. Right away, Sire!"

The small party of guards, fearing for their lives, hurried out to find the trail of the fugitives. It was clear at times to follow, but why were the prisoners heading toward the setting sun, rather than away from it?

"This makes no sense," their leader said, "but it is the only clue we have of their flight."

Jogging at a slow pace, Hanani's company arrived near dawn at their rendezvous point. It offered little in the way of cover, so the group turned a short distance away from the coast toward some sand dunes. The dunes at least would offer a view of the area from their top. The refugees could see any enemies approaching and could also see their companions arriving.

By the time they struggled to the top of the nearest dune, it was daylight. Soon other escapees arrived and spotted Hanani's contingent.

"Let's see," Hanani addressed the arrivals, "we were six groups. How many have arrived?"

"I count four," Commander Elon said. "That leaves two to arrive yet, unless they have been captured."

"Let us wait until the third hour," suggested Hanani. "If they haven't arrived by then, we must move on or we will be captured for sure. We need to find water soon and then something to eat. We can't exist long in this desert without both."

Not long afterward the other two teams arrived.

"Brothers, what took you so long?" Zattu asked.

"We spotted an Egyptian patrol, so hid out for awhile," one of their leaders explained.

After some discussion, the combined group agreed to proceed along the coast, in the hopes of finding an oasis. They intercepted the sea and turned northeastward. The sun beat down on them mercilessly. They were tired, parched and hungry. Finally they spotted a freshwater lake and a stand of date palms.

"Shall we stop here to quench our thirst?" Hanani asked.

"Yes!" the entire company said, almost in unison. They drank deeply, even though the water was lukewarm. They then checked the palms, but found that the dates were not yet ripe. So they reluctantly headed northeastward along the Way of the Sea, ever watchful for Egyptian troops. It would be a hard journey, even under the best of circumstances, and there would be fairly frequent fellow travelers. Not knowing their identity, the refugees could only hide out until they passed. One of their number had been wounded in the battle for Jerusalem, so needed frequent rests.

"Based on a previous journey to Egypt, I calculate about 11 more days to the nearest safe haven, Kadesh-barnea," mentioned Commander Nadab, of the fortress at Debir. "However, we must leave the coast and head southeastward through the desert, in order to reach Kadesh."

"If we can obtain water and food, we can make it," Hanani said. "But we must find both soon."

The troop followed Nadab's advice and turned toward Kadesh-barnea. By evening they had located a small stream winding its way through the harsh Wilderness of Paran. They did find wild grain and plucked all they could manage to eat. Quail abounded, but how could they catch them? One of the commanders said,

"I can throw stones accurately. I will try to hit some of them."

He picked up several smooth stones and threw them with deadly accuracy, bringing down several of the birds. Others joined him, so they finally had 25, enough to feed their entire party. Now all they lacked was a fire. That was no real challenge, because they all knew how to rub sticks together to create a spark. Several gathered up dry grass, piled it up and proceeded to coax a spark to fall on the grass.

"Success!" shouted one and then several. Hanani and others sought out dead limbs from acacia trees and soon had fires going. The feathers were scorched off the birds and they were then put on wooden spits and held over the fires. It took a long time, but finally the carcasses were pronounced ready to eat.

"What a feast!" commented Nadab, after he had led a prayer of humble gratitude to Elohim. They ate ravenously and soon were ready for some much-needed sleep.

"We need to take turns standing guard," Haggi, commander at Hebron, said. "I will take the first watch. Since we are all tired, I will guard us for two hours and then call one of you to replace me. You, in turn, can call the next one."

This routine went on day after day and night after night. Would they never reach the end of that forbidding wasteland? With every step their bare feet sank into the burning sand or were lacerated on jagged rocky outcroppings. When captured, they had been stripped of their sandals. The lack of footwear made for painful progress, step after step after step, blood soaking into the soil beneath each footprint.

To make matters worse, Gamaliel, the wounded commander, was in such agony that he had to be helped along the way and even carried. At one stop he cried out in pain.

"Brothers," he moaned, "leave me here. I am holding you back."

"We will do nothing of the sort!" answered Hanani. We are a team and will continue to be a team, even if we have to carry you all the way to Kadesh."

"Right!" agreed his colleagues.

Finally and painfully slowly they entered the Wilderness of Zin, with rugged mountains, canyons and rocks everywhere, but it was a bit more hospitable than Paran. There was an occasional wadi, bordered by patches of grass and scattered low trees. At each night's stop they made crude lances, selecting straight dead limbs and forming a tip with sharp stones. One evening some of their number climbed atop a higher plateau, where they surprised a hart. Chasing it to a sharp drop-off, they forced it over the cliff.

"Praise Elohim!" the fugitives shouted. "We have meat!"

They soon skinned the animal with sharp stones and cooked some of its flesh. The remaining meat they smoked over a fire, to preserve it. Then, with sinews from the hart they made crude bowstrings. Limber new branches from trees were turned into bows. Arrows were fashioned from straight, thin limbs, sharpened to a point and adorned at the other end by feathers, to give them stability in flight. After a few tries, they found that their bows and arrows sufficed as weapons. So now they had lances and bows, which gave them some security from predators.

"Look there, ahead! Is that not Kadesh-barnea?" their point man came running back to the main group to report. After weeks of tiring journey and encounters only with wild animals, the refugees were overjoyed to see the town's walls. They picked up their pace and soon hailed the gatekeepers. Identifying themselves, they were welcomed into the fortress, burnt brown by the sun, gaunt and tired, but relieved at their delivery from what had appeared often to be certain death.

"Welcome to our city. You must have quite a story to tell," Commander Paltiel told them. "After you have bathed, received new clothing and eaten, we will want to hear of your misadventure and escape."

Nothing but Sand

"Brother, we have a fellow commander who is in critical condition," Haggi said to Paltiel. "Before our needs are provided for, would you see to him?"

"Certainly. We have a good healer here. I will turn your commander over to him. He will be most attentive to his situation."

"Thank you. And now I think we are ready for some decent food and rest on real bed mats."

"Come this way. First, I can tell you are in urgent need of a bath and decent clothing. Then we will see to getting some meat back onto your bones."

The safe-and-sound refugees were given all of the care the fortress could lavish on them. After a real feast, the commander, his staff and the fugitives leaned back on their cushions. Then various commanders in the group, including Hanani, filled them in on their story.

"Great courage and inventiveness, warriors," Paltiel said. "I will see to it that our king knows of this tale. Now, I am reasonably sure that all of you want to get back to your fortresses, commands and families. I am ordering some of my men to escort you and will provide horses for your continued journey. I suspect you have walked far enough for now."

"Thank you," they all shouted, relieved that they would have mounts to ride.

When they were ready the next day to leave, Paltiel dismissed them with a blessing,

"May our great Elohim continue to guide and protect you. Shalom."

"Shalom, Commander, and we thank you again," they echoed.

The former prisoners were in a great mood, as they hurried on their way back to their fortresses. They considered themselves to be the fortunate dead raised to life. Only by Adonai's strong arm had they been protected and guided. Soon they would be home. They separated to their respective fortresses, each embracing the others. They were truly a band of brothers, bound together by all they had endured.

Hanani hurried just as rapidly as he could. Even the Scorpion Ascent held no obstacle to him, after all he had been through.

"Just a little farther and I will be reunited with my Hannah and comrades!" he shouted out to his escort and the canyon walls, his words echoing off them in a myriad of repetitions. When he finally saw Tamar in the distance, Hanani urged his horse into a gallop. His "hated" fortress never looked better to him than it did that instant.

scroll 31
Reunited at Last!

"Hannah! Hannah!" Hanani shouted, as he sprinted toward his desert home and jumped off his mount.

Hannah appeared at the door to her home and stared, incredulous, at the approaching figure. She couldn't believe what she was seeing!

"It can't be!" she muttered. Yet it was! It was her beloved Hanani, returning to her from the dead. She lifted her skirt and ran like a child toward him.

"O Hanani!" She cried, "Hanani, Hanani, my love!" Falling into his arms, she sobbed, "I thought you were dead, but Adonai has brought you back to me."

"I love you, I love you, I love you," he whispered to her between kisses. "I despaired of ever being with you again, but by the grace of our great Adonai, here I am."

"You look so thin, my husband. You haven't been eating well."

"You might say that, my love. There were times when we were fortunate to have even wild grass seeds to eat. Now, how about going with me to the fortress, so I can greet our comrades? And you, companions, come with us. I will see that you and our mounts are well cared for. And then, after reporting in, I propose that we take a walk back to our home. I haven't yet met our child. Is it a boy or a girl?"

"You have a strong and healthy son, my husband. Subject to your approval, we have named him Amran ben Hanani, in honor of both you and your father."

"I couldn't be more pleased."

Reunited at Last!

As they went through the gate, they heard a resounding roar. A lookout had seen Hanani approaching, so had spread the word. The entire company turned out to welcome its commander.

"Praise Adonai!" shouted Joab. "Our great Adonai has brought you back safely to us. Ismaèl, seriously wounded, was able somehow to make it back here. He is still recovering. You will want to greet him and fill us in on your story."

"Thank you, my friend. I will gladly do that, but tomorrow, alright?"

"Certainly. Now get out of here."

"Yes, my brother!" Hanani said with a broad smile. "Please see to my escort. Now Hannah, I'm very much past due to meet my son. Let's go!"

They entered their home and Hannah picked up little Amran, handing him to Hanani. He awkwardly took the baby in his arms and told him what a wonderful little man he was. He continued to croon to his son; that is, until an accident occurred. Suddenly the front of Hanani's tunic was well dampened.

"So," he asked, as Hannah laughed, "Is this how you show respect for your father?"

"Dear husband," Hannah said, "he disrespects everyone equally. You will become accustomed to such happenings."

Then an attractive young maiden entered this tender domestic scene. Looking up, Hannah asked her beloved,

"My dear, do you remember my sister Jemimah? After my mother returned home, Jemimah came to help me."

"Certainly I remember her. Thank you, Jemimah, for being here in my stead."

"It has been my pleasure, Hanani. Welcome home. We thought we would never see you again and were preparing to return to Beersheba."

The women then dismissed themselves to the cooking area and prepared a truly marvelous dinner for their returning man. After he had eaten his fill and Jemimah had taken little Amran off to bed, Hanani drew Hannah to his side on a cushion, held her close and told her some more of his story.

"How awful, my husband! How did any of you ever survive?"

"Only by the grace of Elohim, my little dove, and by His grace I am back where I belong. I have a lot to do to catch up on my duties, and I suspect that my domestic responsibilities have some catching up to do, also. Are you ready to work on them with me?"

"I am more than ready, my hero."

Tamar

    We leave them now to their privacy, as moans of pleasure drift from their mat . . . that is, until an angry war whoop sounds from Amran's crib, shattering their idyll.

Glossary

Abraham: The father of both the Jewish nation through his son Isaac and the father of some of the nomadic peoples through his son Ishmael.

Abijah: A son of Rehoboam and heir to his throne.

Acacia: A hardy tree found in desert regions of Israel, Egypt, Arabia and other neighboring regions.

Ahijah: A prophet of northern Israel who foretold to that God would separate Israel into two kingdoms, giving one to Jeroboam.

Allelu-ya: A Hebrew expression meaning "Praise the Lord."

Amalek, Amalekites: Name of a nomadic nation south of Palestine. The Amalekites were not of Arab background, but of a stock related to the Edomites (consequently also to the Hebrews), which can be concluded from the genealogy in Genesis 36:12 and 1 Chronicles 1:36. They were always warlike toward Israel.

Arabáh: The Arabáh or Aravá is a depression 103 miles long from the Gulf of Aqabá to the southern shore of the Dead Sea. From the Gulf of Aqabá northward, the land rises for 48 miles, reaching a height of 230 m (755 feet) above sea level. Then the land slopes down sharply to meet the Dead Sea, which, at 1,373 feet below sea level, is the lowest point on earth. The Arabáh is very hot and dry, and consequently only lightly populated. King Solomon apparently had copper mines there. The Arabáh was at times under Israelite control and at times under Edomite control.

Glossary

Arad: A fortress village in the Negev of southern Israel.

Araor: Another fortress town in the Negev.

Avdat: A town located south of Beersheba. Site of a beautiful, spring-fed canyon and a Hebrew fortress.

Azariah: He and the remaining list of Solomon's officials are found in 1 Kings 4.

Babustis: Capital city of the 23rd (Libyan) dynasty of Egypt. Also called Tanis. Located on the Tanitic branch of the Nile River.

Beersheba: An important town in the Negev of southwestern Israel. It was built in an oval shape and had a fortress. It dated back to the times of Abraham, when he and Abimelech, a local chieftain, made a treaty of mutual peace and support at Beersheba, which meant "Well of the Oath."

Benaiah: One of Solomon's secretaries.

Bethel: A town famous for having been the earlier site of Jacob's dream of a ladder reaching to Heaven (Genesis 28:10–22). It was also the location of one of the two shrines to golden calves erected by Jeroboam, first ruler of the northern Kingdom of Israel.

Bethlehem: Home village of Boaz and Naomi, as well as of King David, and much later, the birthplace of Jesus. Located about 5 miles south of Jerusalem.

Benjamin: A small tribe adjacent on the north to Judah. The Benjamites were descendents of Benjamin, youngest son of Jacob.

Canaan: The land originally occupied by various small kingdoms and tribes. It was conquered in part by Joshua, some of the judges, Saul and David, thus eventually becoming the nation of Israel.

Carmel: A fortified town west of the Dead Sea in the Wilderness of Maon. Made famous in 1 Samuel 25 by the mean-spirited Nabal, his sudden death at God's hand, and David's subsequent marriage to Abigail, Nabal's widow.

Carmel Hills: The range of hills beginning with Mt. Carmel, jutting out into the Mediterranean Sea, and extending southeastward for some distance.

Glossary

Casemate walls: Double walls surrounding a town or city. These walls were separated by a few feet and often had in the lower section between them storage areas, rooms or dwellings.

Covenant: A binding agreement between a stronger king and a lesser king conquered by the stronger one. In Bible usage, a binding agreement offered by God to individuals and groups, promising blessings in exchange for loyalty to him.

Crater: A large bowl, normally of clay. Also spelled with a k, rather than a c.

Cubit, strong cubit, short cubit: A standard cubit was a measurement from elbow to extended middle finger, about 18–20 inches. The short cubit was from elbow to the beginning of the hand.

Cush, Cushites: Cushites, an ancient people living to the south of Egypt and along the Nile River. Also known as Nubians and Ethiopians. In the 8th century BC Cushite King Piye invaded and conquered Egypt. It was ruled from 719 BC by Piye's brother Shabaka, who also invaded Egypt and set up the 25th dynasty. He subsequently made Memphis his capital.

Damascus: Located to the northeast of Israel and the oldest continuously inhabited city in the world. During the reign of Solomon it was an Aramean or Syrian city under Israel's control.

Dan: One of the twelve sons of Jacob. Also, a town in the far northern region of Israel and the site of the second golden calf shrine erected by Jeroboam.

David: Son of Jesse and great-grandson of Ruth and Boaz. Born in Bethlehem, he became a courageous military leader, the second king of Israel and the father of King Solomon. Known for his creation of many of the psalms in the Bible, for the most part he was an exemplary servant of God.

Debir: A fortress town southwest of Hebron.

Dothan: A town southeast of Megiddo, in the Central Highlands of Israel. Site of Joseph's being sold by his brothers as a slave to Edomite traders.

Ebal and Gerizim: Twin mountains located on either side of the village of Shechem. From these two mountains the Israelites, newly-established in the Promised Land, repeated the words of the Law.

Glossary

Edomites: Warlike descendants of Esau, Jacob's twin brother. Lived south and southeast of the Dead Sea. Their major stronghold was Sela, later made famous by the Nabateans as Petra, the city carved out of rock.

Elohim: A Hebrew name for God. A plural noun, referring to God as Lord, Preserver, Transcendent, Mighty and Strong.

El Shaddai: A name for God, meaning "God Almighty" or "God All-Sufficient."

Ezion-geber: Or Eilat, a seaport on the eastern arm of the Red Sea. Famous in Solomon's days as the home base for his fleet of trading ships.

Feast Days, Feast Celebrations: Three Feast times were mandatory for all Israelites, when they were expected to be in Jerusalem for special sacrifices and other observances. These were Peshach (Passover), Shavuot or hag shavu`ôt, (Feast of Weeks or Pentecost), and Sukkot (Feast of Booths or Ingathering at the end of the fruit harvest). Other special celebrations included Yom Kippur (the Day of Atonement), New Moon, the Sabbath, the Sabbath year (every seventh year) and the Jubilee year (once every fifty years).

Forty lashes minus one: Israelite law limited beating of guilty parties to 40 lashes with a whip. In order never to pass that number, those responsible for the punishment stopped at 39.

Gaza: Philistine city in the southeast coastal region of Canaan and near the Mediterranean Sea.

Gideon: A judge and military commander during the period following the conquest of much of the Promised Land of Canaan by Israelite forces. Read his story in Judges 6 and 7.

Great Sea: The Mediterranean Sea.

Hannah: Our heroine, named after Hannah, one of the two wives of Elkanah and the mother of the prophet and judge Samuel, who gave Samuel to the Lord at a tender age.

Hart and hind: Male and female deer.

Glossary

Holy Place, Most Holy Place: The Holy Place was the first interior section of the Hebrew Tabernacle and Temple. Attended by priests, it housed an altar of incense, a table for consecrated bread and golden candlesticks. Beyond it, and separated by a curtain, was the Most Holy Place or Holy of Holies, into which the high priest entered annually to make atonement for his sins and those of his people. It contained the Ark of the Covenant.

Huppah: A special canopy or arbor constructed for marriage ceremonies. The bride and groom stood beneath it, where they were blessed by the priest presiding over the ceremony.

Ibex: A species of wild mountain goat with long horns curving backwards. Ibex meat was highly regarded by the Hebrews.

Ir-nahash: A small town in the southern Arabáh, controlled in Hanani's day by the Edomites.

Isaac: The heir of Abraham, who became the father of Esau and Jacob, and through Jacob, the people of Israel.

Israel: The new name God gave Jacob. It means, "He struggles with God." The Israelites received their name from him and it still exists in the modern nation of Israel.

Jacob: One of the twin sons of Isaac and grandson of Abraham. Father of twelve sons whose descendants became heads of the twelve tribes of Israel.

Jeroboam: One of Solomon's officials who had rebelled against him and fled to Egypt. Upon Solomon's death he returned to Jerusalem to confront the new ruler, Rehoboam. When the king responded foolishly to the request of Jeroboam and other leaders to lessen taxes, Jeroboam led another rebellion that resulted in the separate nation of Israel.

Jerusalem: The ancient city of Salem which became David's new capital.

Jezreel: A fertile valley at the western end of Mount Gilboa. The city of Jezreel overlooked the whole plain to the north and west. It was the site of King Ahab's summer palace.

Joseph: 11th son of Jacob and his favorite. Sold into Egyptian slavery by his brothers, he arose to be prime minister of that empire and, in that position, saved his people from a famine.

Glossary

Joshua: Interestingly, this name means "savior" and is identical to the named given to Jesus: Yeshua, the Cristos, Savior, the Anointed One.

Judah: One of the southern tribes of Israel and the tribe later forming the bulk of the nation of Judah. Cities such as Jerusalem, Bethlehem, Hebron and Beersheba were located in Judah. The fortress at Tamar was also in Judah.

Jujube: A giant long-lived desert tree. A jujube currently at Tamar is more than 2,000 years old. Its lower branches have drooped to the ground and there rooted, to form more "trees" out of the main trunk.

Kadesh-barnea: A city located about fifty miles east of the Mediterranean Sea and fifty miles southwest of Beersheba. Kadesh means "holy" or "consecrated." Kadesh-barnea is also referred to simply as Kadesh in Scripture.

Keturah: Abraham's wife after Sarah's death (Gen. 25:1–6).

Kidron Valley: A low, steep-sided valley immediately to the east of the city of Jerusalem.

Kosher animals: Animals listed in the Law of Moses that were permitted for food. To be kosher, they had to both have a cloven hoof and chew the cud.

Levites: Descendants of Jacob's son Levi. The Levites were the priestly tribe of Israel.

Mancala: A family of ancient board games played around the world, sometimes called Sowing Games or Count and Capture games.

Megiddo: An ancient city in a strategic location at the head of a pass through the Carmel Ridge, which overlooks the Valley of Jezreel from the west. Solomon built it up as a fortress, complete with stables for his chariot horses. The home area of our hero, Hanani.

Midian, Midianites: Midian was the fourth son of Abraham by Keturah Midian became the father of the Midianites (Gen. 25:2,4; 1 Chr. 1:32), who occupied an extensive desert region in eastern Arabia and around the Red Sea. Moses married Zipporah, the daughter of a Midianite.

Glossary

Moab: A land to the east of the Dead Sea, inhabited by Moabites, a nation descended from Lot, nephew of Abraham. Often antagonistic toward the Israelites.

Mohar: The bride's dowry or gift that the intended husband was required to give to the bride's family.

Moses: Prince of Egypt and long later deliverer of Israel from Egyptian slavery, giver of God's Law on Mt. Sinai, leader of Israel for forty years of wandering in the wilderness.

Mt. Carmel: See Carmel.

Mt. Gilboa: A prominent rounded mountain in the Carmel range, located south of Megiddo. Site of King Saul's final battle and death.

Mount of Olives: A hill just east of Jerusalem and the Kidron Valley. Bethany, the home of Martha, Mary and Lazarus, was just beyond the ridge of the Mount of Olives.

Nabateans: A tribe that overtook the Edomites and settled in their region. Nabatean ware and perhaps a Nabatean fortress have been found in the ruins of Tamar.

Needle's Eye: A very small entrance through the wall of a city. It could only be entered by a person stooping over and could therefore be easily defended.

Negev: Also known as Negeb, a large semi-arid region located to the south and southwest of Jerusalem.

Oryx: An antelope species with long straight or curved horns.

Pace: The average length of stride of an adult male.

Passover: A feast period celebrating the passing of death over the houses of the Israelites in Egypt, so that their firstborn were spared. It was kept annually as one of the required feasts of the Israelites.

Philistia: Land of the Philistines, located in the southwestern region of Canaan and along the Mediterranean coast. The Philistines were descendants of Sea Peoples, probably from Crete, who had attacked Egypt and had been

Glossary

repelled, opting to settle along the southeastern Mediterranean coastal region. The Philistines, occupying five city-states, were sworn enemies of the Israelites.

Phoenicia: A region of city-states to the far northwest of Israel. Tyre and Sidon were prominent among them. The Phoenicians were masters at maritime trading and established colonies elsewhere in the Mediterranean area. They furnished materials and technical skills for the construction of Solomon's temple and palace, and also crews for his cargo ships.

Ramah: Ramah in Benjamin was located near Gibeon and Mizpah to the West, Gibeah to the South, and Geba to the East.

Ramón Crater: A former seabed, hot and dry, with seashells scattered along its sandy and rocky surface. In ancient times, it was necessary to climb up out of it to reach the Negev Highlands, or descend into it to reach the eastern Negev.

Rehoboam: Solomon's son who succeeded him on the throne of Israel. Because of a foolish decision he made regarding taxation, he lost ten tribes to Jeroboam, remaining with only Benjamin and Judah, plus a number of Levitical priests and their families.

Sabbath: Seventh day of the week, which began at sundown on the sixth day, our Friday, and ended at sundown on the seventh day.

Sacred Ark: Ark of the Covenant, a golden box located in the Holy of Holies in the tabernacle and temple. Initially, it held the two tablets of the Law, a jar of manna and High Priest Aaron's rod. Only the high priest could enter the Holy of Holies in the presence of the ark, and then only once a year.

Samuel: A prophet and the last of the pre-kingdom Israelite judges. Against his will, Samuel anointed Saul the first king, then later, due to Saul's disobedience of God's orders, replaced him with David.

Scorpion Ascent: A very steep and perilous climb into and out of the Ramón Crater. The name Scorpion gives a strong clue as to some of the perils encountered on the ascent.

Sela: Stronghold of the Edomites. Later it came under Nabatean control and was further carved out of rock canyon walls and called Petra.

Glossary

Shalom: In Hebrew the word means "peace." It was used both in meeting someone and bidding goodbye.

Saul: A Benjamite anointed as Israel's first king. He turned away from following God's will for him and was rejected as king, in favor of David, from the tribe of Judah. Saul became mentally deranged and finally died a suicide after being wounded in a battle.

Shechem: A Levite city about halfway between Megiddo and Bethel, and located in the center of the western region of Ephraim.

Shekel: A fixed weight in pieces of gold or silver, money as such not having yet been invented in Hanani's day. Ten thousand shekels in gold would have been a huge pile of bullion.

Shema: The Shema is a declaration of faith in one God. The obligation to recite the Shema is separate from the obligation to pray. A Jew was obligated to repeat the Shema in the morning and at night (Deut. 6:7).

Shemaiah: A prophet of God during the time of Solomon and Rehoboam.

Sheol: Hebrew word meaning "The abode of the dead."

Sheshonk: Seschonshis I, also known as Shi-shask, Libyan pharaoh of Egypt's 22nd Dynasty. The first pharaoh mentioned by actual name in the Bible.

Shiloh: A town in the Central Highlands of Israel, located south of Shechem. It was the home of the tabernacle for a period of time during the rule of the judges.

Shofar: A ram's horn used as a trumpet in battle and on other occasions, especially those dealing with feast days.

Sidon: One of the city-states of Phoenicia.

Sinai: A peninsula between Egypt and Arabia/Canaan. Mt. Sinai is in the lower region of the peninsula. The Israelites crossed Sinai in transit to the Promised Land.

Solomon: Son of David and third king of Israel. Known for his great wisdom and vast wealth, but fell into idolatry in his old age.

Glossary

Span: The measurement between outstretched thumb to outstretched little finger.

Spice Road: The caravan route from India and the East Indies through Edom and Tamar, toward Gaza and the coastal route from Phoenicia to Egypt.

Tabernacle: The sacred tent of Israelite worship. Constructed early in their sojourn from Egypt to the Promised Land, it continued in use until Solomon built a permanent temple.

Tamar: A fortress located south of the Dead Sea, at a transition point between the Negev and the Arabáh. Also a junction of the Spice Road and the road from points north to the Red Sea. Several fortresses were constructed, one on top of the other, by Israelites, Nabateans and later, Romans. Tamar is the location for most of the events described in this novel.

Tamarisk: A desert tree surviving, much as does the acacia, on little water.

Tarshish: The ancient name for Spain, the farthest western reach of the world known by the Israelites.

Tel: A mound formed by successive layers of construction at a town or fortress site.

Temple: The sacred place of worship in Jerusalem, first constructed by Solomon in about 950 BC. It was destroyed by the Babylonians in 587 BC, rebuilt after many delays in 515 BC and again essentially rebuilt by Herod the Great from 19 BC onward, with work continuing until 64 AD. It was destroyed for good by the Romans in 70 AD.

Tirzah: A town located directly south of Megiddo and home of our heroine, Hannah.

Torah: The Hebrew word for the first five books of the Bible.

Tyre: A major city-state and maritime port of the Phoenicians. It was located on an island just off the coast of the Great Sea.

Uzziah: A descendant of David and 10th ruler of Judah, following the division between the north and the south at the time of Rehoboam.

Glossary

Watch: The Jews had the nighttime divided into three watches, 6 to 10 PM, 10 to 2 AM and 2 to 6 AM. These were the assigned periods for standing watch on city walls or at a military fortress.

Way of the Sea: A major ancient road running along the Mediterranean Sea to Egypt.

Wilderness of Paran: An extensive, largely desert region in southernmost Israel.

Wilderness of Zin: A sub-region in the northern part of the Wilderness of Paran. Kadesh-barnea was located in this wilderness.

YHVH: Yahweh-sabaoth, the Lord of Hosts and commander of His angels and armies. The tetragrammaton YHVH is the covenant name of God, the self-existent One, the "I am who I am." From YHVH we get the English word, Jehovah, or the transliteration from Hebrew, Yahweh.

Zechariah: Hannah's father.

Zebulon: One of the sons of Jacob and a tribe in northern Israel. Megiddo was located in Zebulon.

Ziklag: A town in the southwestern Negev. Granted to David by the Philistine ruler of Achish.

www.ingramcontent.com/pod-product-compliance
Lightning Source LLC
Chambersburg PA
CBHW071445150426
43191CB00008B/1243